WHO'S
WATCHING
YOU?

Conspiracy Books is dedicated to publishing the truth about all conspiracies, ancient and modern, theoretical and real. Informative, entertaining, subjective and incisive, Conspiracy Books will endeavour to bring the reader closer than ever before to the reality of the conspiracies that surround us.

WHO'S
WATCHING
YOU?

JOHN GIBB

COLLINS & BROWN

First published in 2005 by Collins & Brown
The Chrysalis Building
Bramley Road
London W10 6SP

An imprint of **Chrysalis** Books Group plc

Produced by Conspiracy Books
PO Box 51726, London NW1 9ZH

British Library Cataloguing-in-Publication Data:
A catalogue record for this book is available from the
British Library.

ISBN 1-84340-292-0

1 3 5 7 9 8 6 4 2

Printed and bound in Great Britain by
Creative Print & Design (Wales), Ebbw Vale

Contents

Preface

At 8.45am Eastern Standard Time on September 11, 2001, the world changed – suddenly and for ever. This was the moment when American Airlines flight 11 flew into the North Tower of the World Trade Center, in New York City. Eighteen minutes afterwards, United Airlines 175 struck the South Tower. It was the South Tower that collapsed first, at 9.58am Eastern Standard Time. The North Tower collapsed just thirty minutes later. For the United States of America this was an atrocity of mind-numbing magnitude, inflicted, apparently without warning, by Al Qaeda, then an obscure and underrated, Islamic terrorist organization operating from caves deep in the mountains of Afghanistan. Shocked into action, the US struck back with all its military might to destroy the Taliban Government of Afghanistan that had harboured the perpetrators, and to drive Al Qaeda from its subterranean strongholds.

Alongside this very bloody conflict, however, the US launched a secret war against an invisible enemy – the global terror network made up of Al Qaeda members and supporters. The 9/11 attack had been meticulously planned. The nineteen men who carried it out were well trained, well funded, and had the inestimable advantage of a ready willingness to die for the cause. This combination of money, brains and single-mindedness posed an unprecedented level of danger that, to the US Government, had to be matched with an equally uncompromising reply – at least in terms of civil liberties. The response by the US was the rapid setting up of the Department of Homeland Security and the introduction and enforcement of the Patriot Act, which – together with the fear generated by the attack itself – created paranoia and confusion within the law enforcement and security agencies.

At a stroke, these measures seriously undermined many of the rights and freedoms that had been enshrined in the US Constitution and subsequently upheld through innumerable legal judgments. The US administration threw huge amounts of money into developing systems that could eavesdrop on the public and profile the behaviour of anyone who might be suspected of being an "enemy of the State". It gave rise to a climate of fear in which surveillance of US citizenry could be tightened up and made even more intrusive – and fully justifiable to an American people still reeling from the shock of the Al Qaeda attack.

In Britain, we watched the turmoil in the US and reminded ourselves that we had been through all this before with the Irish Republican Army. But, of course, compared to the global ambitions of Al Qaeda, Northern Ireland amounted to little more than a small, provincial embarrassment. Within only a few months, we were arresting groups of Islamic extremists who were apparently in Britain to murder us all in our beds. In 2005, the United Kingdom Government under Prime Minister Tony Blair sought to make the threat posed by terrorists such as convicted killer Kamel Bourgass sufficient justification to introduce unprecedented new restrictions on civil liberties – indefinite confinement without charge, use of evidence extracted under torture (albeit obtained abroad), warrants issued by politicians rather than judges, and restrictions on access to public buildings and even Parliament itself.

So what is going on? Is the free world under threat or is it all a plot to erode our precious privacy and personal freedoms. This book outlines some of the questions and offers some of the answers. What is undeniable is that we're all being watched. But how closely? And by whom?

Introduction

It's hard to appreciate the impact of a terrorist attack unless you have experienced one yourself. In my case, it was a mixture of farce and embarrassment. The only serious element was that it was the first of a long series of Irish Republican assaults on Britain. We suddenly found ourselves up against bombs made from agricultural fertilizer, stuffed into cars by hopelessly inept but committed middle-class kids, some working off a legacy of oppression and resentment that goes back to the Middle Ages.

March 8, 1973. The day opened with birdsong and sweet spring sunshine. Then, after lunch, a stiff breeze whipped in from the west, ruffling the surface of the Thames and drawing a blanket of grey clouds low over the City. I was strolling down Whitehall Place, heading for the Ministry of Agriculture. London County Council workmen were loading up their van after cleaning the windows of the National Liberal Club on the west side of the street. Big Ben was striking a quarter to three as I made my way down the street toward Whitehall. It took me another five minutes to reach the top of the sweep of steps leading up to the Ministry entrance and I loitered for a moment or two, staring up at the white stone lintel, with its carved relief of shells and sheaves of corn, quarried, I was once told, by convicts from the Verne Prison on Portland Bill.

The bomb exploded at about ten to three. It was a big one, 175lb of agricultural fertilizer, as it turned out. It was packed under the seats of a bronze Hillman Hunter, parked just behind the building. The car had been stolen in Belfast and driven to Dublin three weeks earlier. It had been given new plates and taken on the ferry from Dun Laoghaire to Fishguard and then down to London. Early that morning, Dolours, daughter of old IRA hand Albert Price, a fanatical and ruthless Provisional IRA member ("a Provo"), had driven the Hillman from beneath Dolphin Square and to the Army Recruiting Office in Great Scotland Yard, where it was left. It was six minutes to three when the device was detonated with one of a consignment of Czechoslovakian-manufactured primers donated by the Libyan leader Colonel Khaddafi and clandestinely shipped to the republic. In all, four car bombs had been left in Central London that day by Provo Unit members. At one o'clock a warning was telephoned to the press, giving the registration numbers and locations of the car bombs. The Metropolitan police, not lightning fast at the best of times in those days, managed to find two of the devices and Bomb Squad officers disarmed them. I was a victim of the third. The fourth exploded six minutes later outside the Old Bailey. I heard an echoing metallic thud as I sat on the ground staring at a pool of blood gathering from beneath my right buttock.

The energy of the detonation in Great Scotland Yard was confined by the solid mass of an old mews to the north-east and compressed by vehicles parked in front and behind. The blast found its escape route into Whitehall Place where it erupted, rumbling like a storm beneath the archway over Scotland Place and gathering shards of glass and shredded metal as it came. I was told later that the vacuum caused by the explosion had broken every window in Whitehall Place and that

I had been caught by the edge of it. When I managed to regain my senses after a few seconds, I found myself sitting halfway down the steps with a splinter of glass embedded in me and my hair full of dust and powdered windowpane. I had no clear idea what had happened until much later in the day, when I discovered from the *London Evening News* that I had been struck down by the first bomb of the IRA mainland campaign. The Old Bailey bomb, which had been packed into a green Ford Cortina, injured 186 people. One man died later from a heart attack, which the police claimed had been caused by the trauma of the detonation. When the police arrested those responsible, they would be charged with murder.

I sat on the steps for a while watching policemen running up from Charing Cross and hurrying along the street, pausing only to break the windows of parked cars with their truncheons and shouting to each other in high-pitched voices full of panic and adrenaline. Someone had ordered them to go out and look for suspicious objects in cars. Bomb Squad officers were standing around or sitting in their Land Rovers smoking, while they waited for instructions. It seemed to me that I had been lying on the steps for a long time, although I know it can't have been more than a few minutes, and it was beginning to dawn on me that Whitehall had emptied. The public had run or been herded away from Parliament and the government buildings. Whitehall, Victoria Street, the Embankment and Westminster Bridge were suddenly empty and silent except for the echoing alarm bells of police vehicles speeding past the end of the street. I seemed to be experiencing a feeling of detachment from everything around me even when a wild-eyed, uniformed policeman ran across the road toward me shouting incoherently. He stood over me, and ordered me to get to my feet so that he could search me. His sergeant loped up the steps to restrain him before helping me to stand and walk into the Ministry building.

My legs were unsteady and I felt as if I had been hit in the side of the head by a professional boxer. The marble and mahogany entrance hall was humming and out of register, and I took a cup of tea and asked the police sergeant on duty to tell the commissionaire that I had arrived for my meeting with the Minister, Mr Jim Prior, which was fixed for three o'clock. At the time, I seemed to be the only casualty. But I soon discovered differently. When security staff finally carried me down to a waiting Ministry car, they apologized for the lack of ambulances because all available emergency vehicles had been sent to deal with the injured at the Central Criminal Court. I asked the driver to take me back to the *Sunday Express* where I was working at the time. Without taking his eyes from the road, he said, "Don't be an idiot, son. You're going to hospital."

It was four o'clock when we sped past Horse Guards Parade. The Household Cavalry had already replaced their mounted guardsmen with grim-looking squaddies wearing body armour and carrying assault rifles. There was a feeling of unreality, as if our familiar world had come to an end and nothing would ever be the same again. I learned later from the chatter in the casualty department at Middlesex Hospital that ten Irish men and women had been arrested at Heathrow. Britain had been "closed" and turned into a battlefield and was no longer the playground I had known. It was twenty-five years to the day after George Orwell handed the manuscript of 1984 to his publishers.

Twenty years later, on April 24, 1993, the Provisional IRA drove a truckload of high explosive into the City (or "Square Mile") and blew it up in Bishopsgate, badly damaging the NatWest Tower at 25 Old Broad Street and closing it down. This ostentatious pile had been designed by Richard Seiffert and was completed in 1980 at a cost of £72 million. Fortunately for those who worked there, the building was well built, with a huge concrete core from which the forty-two floors were cantilevered. No one was killed, but the violence and audacity of the attack had a profound effect on the Corporation of London, which ran the City. The result was a determined effort among the Financial Institutions to protect Mammon from the Madmen by investing in the highest possible level of security. The outrage of the men in suits was reinforced by their deep pockets, and the response from the police and security services was immediate. It seemed to be okay to bomb politicians and pub customers, but attacking the City was another matter altogether. There could be no tolerance of terrorists compromising the money and insurance markets, not to mention the integrity of the Old Bailey, the cradle of justice and the greatest court in the Western world.

Within days of the NatWest bombing, a ring of concrete and steel was erected around the Square Mile, and uniformed police stopped and checked every vehicle entering the City. At the same time, cameras began sprouting from the monolithic office blocks, little warts fixed in the walls at seven metres above the ground. Some moved as you passed by, some flashed red to show that they were recording. A monitoring station was built and equipped at Wood Street under the control of Bishopsgate Police Station. Within twelve months, the City of London Police were commanding CCTV coverage of every square inch of road and pavement in the Square Mile. There was not a single court-yard, mews or square that they could not monitor and record, and they didn't even have to rely on the Treasury to find the funds. The surveillance was paid for independently by the banks and financial institutions and the system was designed to their own specifications. Money was no object.

In the early days of IRA brutality, the mainland security services outside London served up a strangely neutered response to the well resourced terrorist force. Intelligence was poor and the Provos soon became unpredictable and ruthless. In the early days of the City surveillance system, the quality of the cameras and tapes was basic and the images were in black and white. There was no facility to zoom in and out, no sound, no numberplate recognition, no capacity to recognize and pick up facial characteristics among pedestrians, no digital archive. There was limited coverage of activity on the underground rail stations, and little skill among the watchers. Visitors to the surveillance centre were treated to a viewing of the film library, which included streakers who, for a bet, had taken to sprinting from The Green Man in Victoria Street to the Bishop's Finger in Smithfield. Police officers, tasked with sitting in front of a bank of television screens and waiting for something to happen, found it difficult and boring and naturally used the equipment to record events that relieved the monotony. The commitment to security among the institutions, however, was uncompromising and determined. The Aldermen pulled out their cheque books, the police were forced into line, and the bankers and insurance salesmen could sleep soundly in their beds once again and turn their full attention back to making a living.

The Corporation boasted that every inch of the Square Mile could be scrutinized by police. Any public unease that this statement might cause the was not considered until it had been made a *fait accompli*. When the civil liberties groups finally woke up and began to ask questions and voice their concerns, they were rebuffed with outrage by the Assistant Commissioner and the Home Secretary. When it comes to fighting terrorism, regard for public sensibilities flies out of the window. The ancient alleyways around the Old Lady of Threadneedle street were now being cleaned up. The whores in Cheapside and the Barbican chose to retire, or moved to Tower Hamlets, Southwark or the West End. While fraud and financial crime remained as common as before, armed robbery, mugging and street violence became forgotten crimes in the City. When IRA atrocities proceeded apace in the provinces and the West End, more resources were pumped into protecting the golden heart of the capital, and the watchers were instructed to upgrade their systems with software that recognized and alerted police to the presence of a stolen car within three seconds of it entering the City.

The City of London surveillance system with its automatic numberplate recognition software has proved a successful car crime stopper and is to be extended throughout the United Kingdom, initially to twenty-three police forces in England. The system will notionally be used to trace the eight and a half million cars that are either untaxed, uninsured or suspected of being connected with criminal activity or terrorism. The cameras are now capable of monitoring three a half thousand vehicles an hour and they will be housed in fixed locations and mounted in police vans. They are looking for motoring criminals rather than bad drivers. However, there are a variety of systems in operation, including one consisting of a consecutive series of hidden cameras that time a vehicle over a mile or so of carriageway. This system is designed to deal with speeding cars that slow down when they know that a camera is just round the corner, because it takes an average of the vehicle's speed over the whole journey. The authorities like it because it does not discriminate in any way. No regard is paid to whether a driver deserves the benefit of the doubt or not. It cannot give a subjective judgment, unlike a police officer in uniform. Either you are breaking the law or you are not.

Surveillance systems and technology improve all the time and there is already nothing to stop the police and security services linking the system to the Swansea-based Driver and Vehicle Licensing Authority (DVLA) database that holds the name and address of the owner of every car in the country. Not only would this enable police to pull in motorists for unpaid parking and speeding fines, but they could also trace their daily movements. The danger for civil liberties is that it allows enforcement agencies – and therefore the State – to build up a comprehensive picture of our movements and behaviour, and to draw conclusions from what they record. The analysis is not carried out by a committee, or a functionary sitting at a desk, but by a computer, which has been programmed to reach its conclusion based on data received from a variety of sources. An example is the Carnivore system, used by the FBI, which records an individual's reading habits sourced from library records and book purchases. Once they know what we're reading, it's a short step to forming an opinion on our political credentials and suitability. And that's the end of liberty.

The routine surveillance of members of the public through the use of closed circuit television (CCTV) becomes even more worrying when combined with other recent developments. The Home Office and security services now routinely employ wiretaps without the need to apply for a warrant from a judge. They are also experimenting with software that is designed to identify the faces of members of the public from a photographic databank sourced from arrest records and from the Passport Office and other government agencies that require photographic identification. The technology is already used by the gaming industry in the United States and is being introduced privately in one or two casinos in London, too. The gaming industry regularly exchanges information about gamblers suspected of cheating. Blackjack and roulette are particularly vulnerable to the professional, and players are watched and recorded all the time. Unwelcome gamblers, blacklisted elsewhere, are covertly filmed and identified as soon as they enter the building and are then refused entry to the gaming floor. The panic that ensues among security personnel when a casino's surveillance system breaks down is dreadful to behold. The accuracy of facial recognition, however, is debatable, unlike DNA and iris recording.

Since the early days of the IRA campaign on mainland Britain of the seventies, and the various domestic terrorist gangs that sprang up in Europe, such as the Red Brigades in Italy and the Red Army Faction in Germany, privacy and data protection safeguards have been routinely set aside during moments of national emergency. Any rules that are bent tend to stay bent long after the apparent threat has disappeared or is shown to be non-existent. For instance, the history of the imprisonment of terrorist suspects at Long Kesh in Northern Ireland in the seventies made it easier for the Home Secretary to imprison Islamic extremists in Belmarsh Prison thirty years later – and to leave them there without trial. The data collected for the proposed Identity Card database will be available to other government agencies such as the Inland Revenue and Customs and Excise. As the perceived threat of terrorism increases, the pressure put on the rule of law by politicians becomes ever more intense. We have already seen intense pressure to do away with the jury system and the presumption of innocence for many crimes, both here and in the United States. How long will it be before a British Home Secretary goes against the wishes of the security services and demands that the rules of evidence be altered to incorporate wiretapping?

The main justification for all these attacks on personal freedoms comes about because, in the shadow of 9/11, the threat of terrorism can be used to justify any extreme measure. When the Government exaggerates or lies about that threat, we enter a dangerous period in our history.

When I was a young man and Churchill was Prime Minister, the idea that he would lie to the nation in order to go to war was inconceivable. He may well have been an old rogue, but there was never any doubt that he had the interests of the nation at heart. He was a fighter and a soldier. He had been brought up to serve his country and had been a prisoner of war in South Africa. Today, although we don't yet seem to care, we are ruled by politicians who put party and personal power before everything else.

The introduction of the Identity Card in the UK is a much bigger deal than we appear to understand. It will mean that the movements and actions of every member of the public can be recorded and stored on security databanks that will be run by private security companies. As technology improves, the time will arrive – sooner rather than later – when a computer file containing our health records, credit rating, overseas travel, voting history and every movement and decision for which we are expected to present a card, will be available to a civil servant and thence to a politician, who may or may not have our interests at heart. It is difficult to understand what advantages such a system will provide to members of the public. If there is a genuine terrorist threat, it is ridiculous to imagine that a committed suicide bomber is going to be deterred by the need to own a small piece of plastic. Politicians talk about ID cards helping to secure our borders against unwelcome intruders, but nobody seems to have thought about the difficulty of the open border between the Republic of Ireland

and the UK. On the other hand, knowledge is power and today's politicians will find a way out of the dilemma. The Identity Card database, and all the associated government agency databases that go with it, will give the State an unprecedented ability to poke its nose into our private lives.

Since the destruction of the World Trade Center, fear of terrorism has become part of our daily political diet, the *raison d'etre* for countless examples of political excess. The men in the shadows, the technology experts and their political masters now have a big say in our lives, both here and in the United States. It is in the nature of the watchers to collect and store all they can about us and to keep it secret. That is what this book is about.

Chapter One: You Shop, We Watch

Years ago, daily life used to be an uncomplicated affair. You went to work, drove into town to pick up your fruit and vegetables at the greengrocer, bought bread at the baker, and chose a joint of beef at the butchers. The notion that one day you might be filmed on your way to work, photographed in your car, monitored as you chose and paid for your groceries, had your loyalty digitally recognized and your personal database updated when you paid your bills, would have been inconceivable. But it has now happened. Virtually everything we do is recorded and saved. And we don't seem to care. Perhaps it is because we don't realize how much of our privacy we are giving away every day. Anyway, we haven't done anything wrong so we've nothing to fear. Or have we?

During the last thirty years, the fire-walling of city centres in an attempt to guard against terrorism has grown steadily and almost without restriction, and it has had a dramatic effect on street life in the UK. No one seems to know for sure exactly how many surveillance cameras there are watching us as we go about our business in the cities, but even conservative estimates put the number in the millions. Clive Norris, Professor of Criminology at the University of Hull, recently published his own estimate. He put the number at three million working surveillance cameras recording public behaviour in the

United Kingdom. Simon Davies, director of the campaigning group Privacy International says, "It is hard to be accurate. Not all systems are registered under the Data Protection Act, but we reckon a conservative estimate is between two and three million individual units. Or around two for every thirty members of the population." It has been claimed that the average Briton is filmed by surveillance cameras up to three hundred times a day. This makes Britain the most watched society on earth. The fact is, we just don't know how many times we are snooped on.

We know that we are being filmed as we travel by rail, when we're driving, in supermarkets, garages and banks, while we watch a game of football, use an ATM, exercise at the gym, go into court, and walk through the town centre. But none of us can possibly have any idea of precisely how many times we are filmed covertly by the police or security services, or illegally by private individuals for financial reasons. There can be no hard figures for covert surveillance, but so what? The official intrusion everywhere you go is worrying enough to make you self-conscious as, for example, you wait for a bus and glance up to see a camera pointing in your direction. Just keep your eyes open as you stroll past the shops in any busy urban high street if you want to get a picture of who is recording your journey and why.

Most retail businesses belong to associations that exchange surveillance data. When required, they will co-operate to track certain individuals for long periods of time and produce a complete digital record of where they went during the time they spent in the high street. There are many ways that people can be tracked.

Kensington High Street in West London, for example, is one of the most watched streets in the capital. It's nearly a mile of solid, prime location; a pleasant street, once the haunt of rich widows and their poodles but now a shoppers' paradise; home to the offices of the *Daily Mail* and numerous embassies. Start at the Royal Garden Hotel and make your way toward Holland Park. If you glance up at the walls around the hotel reception area, above the heads of the people milling around waiting to check in or pay their bills, you will see half a dozen little boxes hanging there. They are hiding the mobile lenses of remotely controlled cameras.

The Royal Garden is one of the top London hotels. Heads of State, international businessmen, spies, mercenaries, and rich and eccentric celebrities come to stay there. When they've checked in, they want to be able to relax in their rooms and think about having some fun. But they also want to know that they are safe and secure. The managers of the world's biggest hotels know more secrets than most of us. They have to cope with the idiosyncrasies of presidents and dictators, of film stars, rock musicians and drunken writers, and they must keep quiet about it afterwards. They must also make sure that their guests feel they have nothing to fear from the moment they wander past the uniformed commissionaire guarding the entrance. So hotel managers make sure that everyone coming into the building is filmed, and they continue to keep an eye on visitors and guests alike until they leave again.

Just to the east of the hotel is Palace Avenue and Kensington Palace Green. The elegant drive up to Kensington Palace is bordered on one side by Kensington Gardens and on the other by Kensington Palace Gardens. When you stroll outside the hotel and glance along the east wall, cameras and sensors sprout like eyes and ears covering the access to the royal apartments. Razor wire has been attached along the top of the wall to stop anyone trying to damage the equipment or gain a vantage point during a demonstration. It was at this end of Hyde Park that mourners left mountains of flowers in the days following the death of Diana, Princess of Wales. It's a sensitive corner of the United Kingdom. There are yet more cameras across the road, in Bar Cuba, where tourists nip across from the hotel to enjoy a slightly more *risqué* and affordable drink.

A few yards further west, Kensington Palace Gardens is protected by uniformed guards. The tree-lined boulevard is open to walkers but off-limits to cars, unless they carry diplomatic plates, and to all tradesmen, unless they have special clearance. Many of the big diplomatic missions are here, including the Russian Embassy at the north end. There are anti-tank blocks in front of some of the buildings to deter car bombs, and satellite dishes poke up above the roofs and the branches of the plane trees. The tree-lined avenue bristles with surveillance cameras and radio antennae, while armed police patrol up and down, a highly visible deterrent to anyone thinking of protesting outside the Japanese embassy.

If you decide to treat yourself to a coffee on the Edwardian, marbled ground floor of Barkers, on the other side of Kensington High street, you will find kids tapping into laptops and talking on their mobiles. Upstairs, in the towering Northcliffe House, are located the offices of the *Daily Mail*, *Mail on Sunday* and the *London Evening Standard*. With an ease born of long familiarity, the journalists sitting at their desks are able to listen and watch all the communications traffic flickering up from the café below and even from the hotel. Surveillance and security is high and overt in the offices of Associated Newspapers, and the staff are routinely filmed on CCTV. Bags and briefcases are searched and all offices and corridors are dotted with cameras to record what is going on. Journalists are notorious for testing the system. When the government banned gun clubs and made hand guns illegal, one of the first reporters into the building on the day the Act became law placed a large (deactivated) Webley Service revolver on the news desk and said he'd found it in the lift. Security was increased throughout the Associated building shortly afterwards. The company has a substantial security force, not simply because of the political implications of what they do, but because of the secrets they keep but choose not to reveal. Knowledge is everything to a national tabloid newspaper and it is an accepted fact that many of the editors and executives of the company have the power to ruin or seriously embarrass some of the most powerful men in Britain.

Knowledge is also important further down the street, in the Kensington branch of Marks and Spencer, one of the company's key London stores. Outside on the pavement, hordes of women and children are milling about in a disorganized and noisy rabble. They are Eastern Europeans speaking in their own tongue. The children seem to be out of control and the women wear long burkas and headscarves. We will return to them soon.

Unlike other retail businesses, M&S do not, as a matter of course, attach security tags to their merchandise, relying instead on camera surveillance, the overt presence of uniformed guards, and plain-clothed store detectives. It's an effective system. The network of big London stores maintains close links between each retail outlet and reports the movement of any groups of customers considered suspicious. The skill of M&S security and its ability to pursue theft successfully is well tried and tested. When a group of potential shoplifters and pickpockets disperses from Kensington, the stores along Oxford Street are waiting for them. The shops have to rely on their own experience and communications network because communication between the police divisions is not considered fast enough.

To many discriminating shoppers, the stores of Kensington and Chelsea have an air of genteel respectability and calm that is preferable to the frantic retail mania of Oxford Street, a mile or so to the northeast. Less apparent is their impressive record of success against organized theft. The struggle against retail crime never stops and so the surveillance of customers is constant. Everyone is watched entering and leaving and recorded as they walk through the store. The huge amount of investment and thought that has gone into the Marks and Spencer security systems would no doubt be a surprise to us all. The business ends of surveillance cameras all tend to look the same, of course, but there's more to surveillance than that. When you walk into the security monitoring rooms you won't find ranks of screens and bored security guards waiting for the end of their shift. Each store has dozens of working cameras and they are monitored by highly trained individuals sitting behind a large, single screen using the best system money can buy. The technology is known as "neural", which means that the digital cameras are able to distinguish suspicious activity from "normal" behaviour and then channel it to the operator. The software isolates the relevant section of film and prioritizes it so that the monitor will instantly see what is happening, track the people involved and be able to call for assistance from security staff on the shop floor. It is quick, effective and incredibly expensive, but it is the future of surveillance.

Because neural surveillance can isolate particular threats from otherwise acceptable scenarios, it is revolutionizing the art of security monitoring. There are numerous advantages, not least in the way it dispenses with unmanageable banks of screens and a mass of confusing information. The average attention span of police officers operating the huge bank of cameras in the City of London Police CCTV headquarters at Wood Lane was considered to be no more than twenty minutes. Nothing escapes the neural cameras and the "proactive prevention" system that supports them and is able to sift the information they receive and flash it to the monitor screen. Everything that appears on the neural screen is relevant. The single operator required by the system works alone in a command centre remote from the site that is being watched. He or she sits in a spartan chamber with a single, large, wall-mounted screen to which a series of images can be transmitted, each one with its own priority code. The room is softly lit, the operator sits on a comfortable high-backed chair behind a table which holds a bank of telephones.

This versatile system has many other applications, apart from its uses in the retail sector. For example, imagine a rambling, Georgian country house in England, lying in a thousand acres of rolling pasture and woodland, with formal gardens surrounded by a high brick wall three metres thick at the base and topped with razor wire. The four main gateways into the park are electronically controlled. The perimeter of the grounds and the exterior of the house are littered with surveillance cameras and sensors. The interior is similarly secured with small dome cameras, each of which is set to operate with a pre-programmed system. All material recorded by the cameras and sensors is transmitted to the remote monitoring facility where it is filtered and assessed by the system. Each camera records and analyses activities in a precisely defined area. The cameras are capable of integrated "dynamic leading edge" motion detection, tracking and behaviour analysis. This means that if or when an anomaly of any sort is picked up, details are flashed to the control room where the watcher, in front of a large, pin-sharp, wall-mounted screen, can activate the appropriate response.

Each camera is programmed to accept a range of activities within its area. It isolates and records anything that it has been tasked to consider suspicious and filters out everything else. For instance, a man enters the car park at the rear of the property. He is carrying a bag that he places on the ground beside a parked vehicle. He then turns and walks away, leaving the bag behind. The system immediately registers a threat and informs the controller who is asked to make a judgment. The bag is highlighted and cross-hatched on the screen so that the monitoring eye is immediately directed towards it and the operator can instantly see what and where the problem is. The system provides him with a complete film record taken before and after the incident, allowing him to examine the bag and the person who has apparently abandoned it in minute detail.

The system is called Spectiva. It records both audio and broadcast-quality video and is able to pick up and isolate conversation from over a wide area. The watcher is given every detail he needs to help him make the decisions necessary in order to analyse and deal with what has been recorded. If the intruder had put the bag on the ground for a moment or two and then picked it up and continued on his way, the system could have been programmed to ignore him. The camera system has been programmed to act on a huge range of possibilities suggested by the security company that installed it. For instance, if it is night-time and a figure runs across the car park, or enters the orbit of surveillance and crouches down behind a car, the incident will be picked up and instantly flashed to the watcher. If it is daylight and a child runs across the scene, perhaps a regular occurrence, the system can be programmed to ignore it. If someone appears to be carrying a weapon, the camera will recognize it and respond accordingly. As soon as the behaviour has been analysed, the system will continue to track the subject. Irregular clothing, a balaclava or body armour can be recognized and the appropriate response put into effect. Facial recognition technology has made it possible to set up the camera in such a way that it will register the profile or physical characteristics of any known and unwelcome visitors spotted in the house and grounds. However, this technology is still in the early stages of development and can be fooled by the use of clothing or glasses to obscure the face.

In the case of a private house in the middle of a large estate in the English countryside, the priority is likely to be the security of the family and their property, and the system may have been installed on the insistence of the family's insurers. I first experienced the efficiency of neural security at a private house in Hampshire. The system had been installed by a leading specialist surveillance company called CSS, based in Southampton. The house owner took great delight in demonstrating how he was able to monitor the property from anywhere in the world, via his laptop or hand-held "palm" computer. For example, using wireless technology and his laptop, he is able to communicate with and control his cameras from a hotel room in Tokyo. If he wants to, he can then follow any anomalies thrown up by the neural system. His Italian-designed "Cieffe" installation provides full remote video viewing and remote control on a virtual video desktop. Watching the system in operation while sitting in a bar in The City in the company of the householder, I was able to read the small print on his car's tax disc filmed by a camera mounted on the back wall of his house one hundred metres away from the vehicle. However, the facility to intercept the system and keep an eye on his home and family is solely for the householder's peace of mind because the surveillance is monitored twenty-four hours a day by CSS personnel with whom he can be in contact at the touch of a button.

CSS had privately assessed the vulnerability of the house in the country before advising the owner. They fitted complete but unobtrusive perimeter detection security with proactive CCTV that transmits signals to a central monitoring station. The company employs trained operators with the facility to respond immediately to any threat to the house or its contents. Roberto Fiorentino, who runs CSS Security in Southampton, designs bespoke security systems. He said, "We are able to do what the police are often unable to do, which is protect vulnerable locations and prevent serious crime." For instance, in the case of a full-scale attack on a property, the information is selected by the system and displayed accordingly in a selection of prioritised images on the screen, giving the watcher a complete picture of the assault. As a private agency, CSS are not hamstrung by bureaucratic reporting systems but they are trained in the Data Protection Act and all other legislation that governs the presentation of evidence in court. The neural technology used in surveillance is seen by the industry as preventative rather than reactive and is a giant step forward in safeguarding property.

The ultimate aim of systems like the one devised by CSS is to prevent crime in public places. In the US, work on linking neural search, motion detection and motion tracking, with techniques such as facial recognition and global positioning satellite (GPS) technology has been in progress for two years as part of an initiative by the Department of Homeland Security. Their goal is to develop a system that can be applied to a crowded street to prevent a terrorist attack.

Neural surveillance technology is constantly being improved

and reduced in price and staff are receiving more sophisticated training in using it. It will soon be installed by all large retailers and cross-referenced with databases of known thieves. It is no wonder the retail trade is interested in security developments that select what they want to watch and so reduce manpower. During weekends in busy times of the year, the crowded floors of the big stores in the West End are the battlegrounds for retail guerrilla warfare, with intelligence on known and suspected thieves flashed from retailer to retailer across the West End. At peak times throughout the day, police units patrol up and down the street and through the underground station. During the summer months, the stores in Kensington are routinely visited by groups of thieves, many flying in from Eastern Europe and The Balkans. They work in small groups. The front line often consists of women and children supported by men in fast cars cruising up and down the street. Sub-teenage girls and boys will have been trained to be expert at pick-pocketing (also known as "dipping"), evasion and distraction. They carry false identities to try to persuade the police and store detectives that they are underage, and they pretend not to understand English. They operate in teams and are fast on their feet. Escape routes are meticulously planned and rehearsed.

In an attempt to tackle the threat such thieves pose, as soon as there is the merest hint of trouble, or a known criminal is recognized, every store in the street and the police retail crime units at Kensington and Notting Hill are immediately alerted. Several major store chains are now testing facial recognition surveillance as a way of identifying and targeting habitual thieves. It is the Holy Grail of security systems but is still a long way from proving its reliability.

Today, London is the most heavily watched city in the world. In addition to the two million CCTV cameras, there are eight police surveillance helicopters – with two more on the way – which are capable of carrying armed squads quickly to any location in the capital. Heavily patrolled security zones have been created – some more intensively policed than others, according to their perceived vulnerability. The bobby on the beat with his truncheon and whistle has become a distant memory. The modern community copper rides a fast bicycle fitted with state-of-the-art communications systems and offensive and defensive equipment.

The system works. I recently went out on patrol with two members of the City of London Police Bike Unit in Aldersgate, where they spotted an elderly gent walking purposefully in a southerly direction. "I know him," said one of my companions, a muscular constable in Dayglo yellow with a stab jacket and a belt sagging with mace spray, baton, taiser and first aid kit. "He's a jammer," he said, "blocks up telephone boxes with bits of plastic and comes back later to collect the cash. I pulled him up a couple of years ago." He called the CCTV control unit on the radio fitted to his helmet. "There's an old guy in a green raincoat walking down Aldersgate. He's fifty yards south of Long Lane, can you get him up on the system?" Within twenty seconds the man was being monitored on camera, close up and pin sharp, in the surveillance room at Wood Street. We followed at a distance while the watchers recorded him turning into Grubb Street and wandering down to Cheapside, where he stopped to stand and stare in a shop window. The police went over to have a word with him while I watched. A third cyclist, a woman constable, materialized on the pavement beside them, although I couldn't see where she had come from. After a couple of minutes, another member of the squad glided to a halt at the kerb. The street was suddenly full of cycle cops.

There was no police aggression, all were friendly and polite, but we'd been following the man for thirty minutes and he'd been filmed covertly and in great detail from Aldersgate to Cheapside. He claimed to work in Finsbury Square and said he was in the habit of taking a walk every lunchtime. But he had been picked up before and as one constable said later, "If he was up to anything, he'll think twice about it in future. We've got his name and address." What this also meant was that the minor incident was now recorded and the man's facial characteristics had been secured on the police databank where they can be recalled at the press of a button and added to their facial recognition database. The subject of this entertaining but forgettable episode had no idea that his lunchtime stroll has been recorded for posterity and that his image can now be called up on a computer screen, not just in London but soon in any country with whom we have an agreement – even after he is long dead and buried.

The City of London surveillance system with automatic numberplate recognition software will soon be extended to twenty-three police forces in England, and then throughout the UK. The system will notionally be used to trace the eight and a half million cars that are either untaxed, uninsured or suspected of being connected with criminal activity or terrorism. The cameras are now capable of monitoring three and a half thousand vehicles an hour and they will be both housed in fixed locations and mounted in police vans. There are no guarantees whatsoever that use of the cameras will be restricted to finding "genuine" criminals.

Surveillance technology improves all the time and already there is nothing to stop the police and security services linking the system to the DVLA database that holds the name and address of every registered car owner in the country. This would not only allow arrests for unpaid parking and speeding fines, but would also enable them to trace motorists' daily movements. The danger for civil liberties is that it encourages the law enforcement agencies and therefore the State to build a picture of our behaviour and to draw conclusions from what they record.

While The City of London is probably one of the most professionally watched and guarded urban landscapes in the world, Kensington isn't really any different from any other high street in the UK. Walk along it and you will be constantly monitored by one camera or another. Enter a shop or restaurant and a new system takes over. All around you, there's a struggle going on between the retailers and the underworld, and you are being dragged into it because you happen to be there spending money. By law, your image must be scrubbed from the system after thirty-one days, but there's no one to check that this rule is enforced. When you use your credit card to pay for your purchases at a till and pass over your loyalty card, the transaction is timed so that there's a record of you on film that can be merged with the details on your cards. The store owners can quickly find out where you live, who you bank with, how many children you have, and much more besides, just by looking at their tapes and comparing them with the cashier's records.

You have to be careful what you say in the street nowadays as well, because when it's picked up from your mobile, it can be analysed and tied to you as an opinion, and you could finish up on a list that associates you with characters regarded as undesirable by the State. It is not just the intelligence gatherers you should be concerned about but many others, including the British media. Genuine "private conversation" without any possibility of being overheard has become a forgotten dream. There is no longer such a thing as a secure telephone, the internet is wide open to interception, emails have become everybody's property. Unless you stand near a waterfall surrounded by a cordon of deaf security men who have been body searched for wires and have formed a tight circle round you with a diameter of at least two hundred metres, there is no guarantee that the confidential chat with your friend or your friend's wife will remain secure. The head of MI5 communicates with the British Prime Minister by means of handwritten briefings delivered by courier to the House of Commons. Even if you employ all the precautions known to man, you cannot guarantee your privacy. There may be a listening or a tracking device somewhere in the ground beneath your feet or in a nearby bush. Perhaps, a satellite filming you or a little air-born bug hovering somewhere in the vicinity that can either listen to you, or monitor the movements of your mouth and translate it into speech.

Mobile phones are banned from private clubs, courts, businesses and political meetings, not just because they're irritating, but because they may be fitted with cameras and voice recorders that are capable of grabbing covert photographs and video clips. Most modern mobile phones have a recording capability sensitive enough to pick up conversations nearby. Miniature, digital, voice-activated recorders such as the Olympus DS330 can be bought on London's Tottenham Court Road for a hundred pounds and tucked away in a pocket, where it will record conversations in a noisy pub and cancel out the background chatter. Although surveillance networks and wiretapping are regulated by the Data Protection Act and Human Rights legislation, nobody knows how many private individuals or companies are operating watching and listening devices to record your activities. How many hotels regularly run a security sweep on their bedrooms for bugs and miniature cameras? Hardly any. Call many of the big London venues and they will hire a specialist anti-bugging crew to fix it for you – if you request it. But it will be prohibitively expensive. They would much rather that you arranged it yourself, however, because they can't guarantee to make their rooms secure and if you *are* bugged, you might hold the hotel responsible. How often would you have to have the room swept? Once, twice a day? And can you guarantee that the security company you hire to check out your bedroom is efficient enough to pick up the fibre optic lens hidden behind the bathroom mirror, and isn't working for someone else? Even an internal sweep for bugs may not be enough. The Sentinel long-range listening device can be trained on a bedroom window and is designed to pick up vibrations and turn them into sound waves. Anyway, how do you stop a journalist with all the most expensive technical equipment he can lay his hands on from overhearing your conversations if he really wants to? His employers will have the resources to acquire more sophisticated equipment than intelligence services can even dream of.

Elizabeth Hurley, like most A-list celebrities, has been bugged many times. "I don't know a famous person who hasn't had their conversations tapped," she said recently. "Everyone has everything searched for bugs the whole time. We all have what's known as drug dealer's phones, with no footprint or listed number, but I've had ordinary landline phone conversations tapped, so I don't talk on the phone any more. I have to meet someone standing on a bridge if I want to have a private conversation. I've even had my hotel room bugged. There's a lot of money at stake for these losers who have no other way of making a living."

Bugging celebrities is not a new phenomenon. Koo Stark once told me that her phone was tapped when she was going out with the Duke of York. "I knew someone was eavesdropping on our telephone calls because the *Daily Mail* printed details of a conversation that nobody could possibly have known from any other source. It was a serious problem because we knew the device was not in the house, so the security service sent some surveillance experts round and they unearthed a bug on the landline beneath the street outside, about twenty metres away from where I lived in a mews north of Belgrave Square. I was certain at the time that it was part of the surveillance organized by David English at the *Daily Mail*. He was desperate to know everything he could about us. It's strange, when you realize that you've been spied on, you become ultra cautious about where you talk to people. Nowhere is safe."

Celebrities might become even more paranoid, with good reason, if they discovered that it is often the police who are giving information to the media. Early in 2005 a ring of ex-Metropolitan police officers, including a control room worker, plus several private investigators, were all convicted of selling vehicle registration numbers and other information obtained from the Criminal Records Office (CRO). The ring had passed on details of television celebrities, as well as details of the driving convictions of a coach driver who had been involved in a crash in France. The intelligence may seem trivial, but it was used to back up speculative tabloid stories. It showed how easy it is to break the rules and that a simple piece of information can be used to add a veneer of truth and add weight to a weak news story in order to make it publishable. For example, the details of the owner of a scooter used to transport a trade union leader around London during industrial disruption on the London underground was passed on to Paul Marshall, a communications officer in a South London Police Station. He, in turn, gave the information to a former policeman, Alan King, who sold it to a journalist. During the trial, the judge remarked that the security of confidential information depends on the trustworthiness of the large number of police officers who handle it. The trial, at Blackfriars Crown Court, in which the four men were convicted, showed that there is a lively market in confidential police material. This will increase as the police computer becomes bigger and more accessible to hackers and cyber-terrorists.

So, while you were shopping in Kensington you were being filmed and your financial transactions were recorded. Now it is time to go home. At Kensington High Street underground station, next door to Marks and Spencers, twenty-five cameras record the comings and goings. As the passengers thread their way through the turnstiles using their Oyster smart cards, they leave an indelible data trail behind them. Police from Transport for London and Kensington Police station in Earls Court Road mingle with the crowds of commuters. The police on the ground are constantly fed information from the watchers via their dedicated radio network as they look for dippers dispersing throughout the tube network.

A tour of any busy street is bound to generate a feeling of nervousness once you begin to realize just how many signals and traces are humming through the air around you. Every time you use a credit card, smart card or mobile, or press the key fob to unlock your car, your exact position in the universe is logged and recorded and your movements and behaviour can be established and followed in great detail. Take a simple walk down a street in West London and you will see sensors absorbing information and transmitting it to public and private databases. Once the data has been recorded it can be shared instantly with the information industry and law enforcement. The electronic footprints we leave behind us have changed our lives forever. Yet most of us are unaware of this fact and so find it difficult to appreciate that we have never existed in this type of environment before.

There is a maxim in the computer industry known as Moore's Law. This states that computer power doubles every twelve months. So there will be plenty of silicon muscle available to process and analyse all that personal data. So now *They* have the knowledge, what will *They* do with it? And who are *They* anyway?

Chapter Two: They're Marking Your Card

Shopkeepers don't rely solely on cameras to find out about us, as we stroll about their stores or pay for our purchases at the checkout. We're willing participants in their quest for information, because we give them all the data they need to build up a meticulous record of ourselves – and we do it for peanuts, year after year. We allow them to see how advertising affects our buying habits, how sensitive we are to product price rises, cut price offers, new product launches and store layouts. They learn whether we're male or female, single or attached, young or old, pregnant or a parent, sporty or sedentary. The industry encourages us to exchange our privacy for a 1 per cent discount. And as they piece together a detailed portrait of us on their database, they learn more about us than the Government knows.

My mother died at a great age, and afterwards, when I was going through her little pile of personal possessions and rummaging through her handbags, I discovered that she had six supermarket bonus cards in her wallet. I knew she enjoyed using them. During the last years of her life, I would take her shopping every weekend because it was a day out for her. After she had found every item on her shopping list and we headed for the checkout, the girl on the till would ask her if she was "a club member" and my mother would make a great fuss of looking for her card and handing it over. She approved of her cards for two reasons. First, she felt that if she hadn't got one she would somehow be missing out; second, she liked to think that she belonged to a club. She never claimed any of the discounts owing to her, as far as I know. I don't think she even read the letters she received from the store. But she came from a generation where thrift was a virtue and collecting bonus points was a way of saving money, even if she didn't actually claim it. It was her duty to be prudent. Her relaxed attitude to it all was not reflected by the retailers she patronized throughout her life.

By the time she died, her siblings had been dead for many years and she had only her immediate family and her carers for company. I discovered that, for many years, she had saved all her letters and kept them in boxes. It was mostly a depressing collection of junk mail, personal acceptance of her non-existent application for "free" platinum credit cards, countless offers of loans, "helpful suggestions" for freeing up some equity on her house so that she could afford a world cruise or a new conservatory, and much more like this. Week after week, year after year, the offers had flooded in. And, of course, there were also the countless times she had won a "Major Cash Prize". All she had to do to claim it, no strings attached, was to "call this number". There – in letters far too small for her old eyes to see – it said, "Calls charged at £5 a minute for the first three minutes." She never fell for any of these scams, however, although every year thousands of old ladies do. As I went through her piles of gaudily printed offers, I found myself wondering what safeguards there are for the elderly and vulnerable and who is there to protect their privacy?

Who knew where she lived and that she was an old woman who owned her own house? Did they know that she had never been in debt during her long life? Apart from her immediate family, the people who knew most about her were the proprietors of the shops she visited. This is because, years ago, she had filled out applications for their loyalty cards and, in doing so, had given away all her personal details. She had continued to give information to them from that point on and had had no idea that what she had written on the form would go any further. Millions of us fall for the soundbites: "Every little helps", "You know it makes sense", "Look after the pennies and the pounds will look after themselves", "Waste not, want not", and "A stitch in time saves nine". Only one of these moralizing axioms is not a relic of traditional Victorian home-spun wisdom, and it's the first. "Every Little Helps" is actually a slick little scrap of advertising copy that defines the philosophy of the Retail Club "loyalty" card, a marketing and intelligence extravaganza that the company describes grandly as an "entire concept". The average retail "loyalty club" embraces the warm feeling of club membership, while helping us all to save money at the same time. A lifetime of grocery shopping adds up to hundreds of little bonuses, particularly if we shop at the same supermarket for everything we need and can answer "yes" to the nagging question, "Have you got a Tesco/Safeway/Boots/Marks and Spencer/Target/Metro store card?" every time you nip out to buy a kilo of sausages. Maybe you use your Nectar card at Sainsbury's, Debenhams, BP and Vodafone, in which case almost every commercial transaction you undertake throughout your life could earn you points. And what do points mean? All together now, POINTS MEAN PRIZES.

Of course, it's not that simple. Stand at the checkout in any large supermarket and look around you. This is a large, bustling space that is carefully designed to be a familiar and friendly corner of your world. Your groceries are totted up and paid for, perhaps, with your Visa card. Your loyalty is acknowledged with a swipe and a smile from the checkout girl, and you wheel your goods out to the car park past the security guard and the shoplifting sensors. You don't want to know that somewhere up above you, the transaction has been filmed on digital CCTV, the payment recorded and timed and the image of you and your face recorded on the database with the details on your loyalty card. The store now owns aspects of your identity that would make any secret policeman green with envy.

Loyalty cards are the modern refinement of Green Shield Stamps, a savings scheme launched way back in the 1950s. Under the scheme, you were given Green Shield Stamps whenever you made a purchase, and you stuck them in a book until you had enough to redeem them. The more you saved, the bigger the reward. Green Shield Stamps were good for you because they taught you to save and be thrifty and they were reassuring because, in those days, stamp collecting was a popular hobby that everyone understood. Stamp collecting was good for Green Shield too, because they sold their little green stamps to the supermarkets and provided the rewards. The problem with Green Shield stamps was that the retailer got very little out of the sale, other than their customers' loyalty, and we all know that there's no such thing as a free lunch. Finally, it dawned on the resourceful grocery trade that they could save money by rewarding their customers' loyalty themselves and burying the cost in the marketing budget. Then it occurred to them that, not only would they save money, but, by recording transactions onto a central computer, they would build up a database of their customers' shopping preferences that would become a priceless resource as time went on.

The concept of loyalty cards seems eminently sensible. The business gets your loyal custom and you get points, air miles or vouchers. Sadly, however, it's a little more complicated than that. If, for example, you move into the Home Counties and shop at Shopco three times every week, you will be made constantly aware that owning a club card will bring you a cornucopia of benefits. You will not be able to resist joining the club and will soon get into the habit of handing your card over every time you go shopping. Every till in every store is linked to the club card database and the result is that every basket of provisions you buy is registered and researched until a detailed picture has been built up about you. If you were to be presented with this analysis of yourself after a few years of "loyalty" you would possibly find it alarming, if not defamatory. But there's not much you can do. The "suits" in the faceless office blocks at HQ turn the incontrovertible facts gleaned from your shopping basket into the flesh and blood of their creations. As far as they are concerned, you are what you buy, and the profile they create from your card is accurate down to the last stock cube.

When you apply for their loyalty card, you are given a "Charter" that guarantees that your details are safe with Shopco. It also promises that if you indicate that you don't want to be contacted for research, they won't bother you. They also affirm that the company complies with the Data Protection Act (which is a legal obligation anyway). Your application form requires that you fill in your personal details including name, address, age, and the age of everyone living at your address. You must also fill in household details, dietary needs and contact information, including email, mobile phone, and so on.

In return, you will be sent a card enabling you to earn one point for every £1 you spend in store, and you will be able to take advantage of special offers on new lines, plus bonus points. Shop "on-line" and you'll make even bigger savings. Each point you earn is worth 1p or 1 per cent, and you can choose to take your rewards as soon as they become available or whenever you decide to cash them in. You can leave them to accumulate for years, if you wish. There are people registered on supermarket databases with thousands of pounds' worth of reward points owing to them. The snag: points don't attract interest. On the American Express database there are millions of dollars' worth of outstanding travellers' cheques still unused years after the holiday they were drawn for is no more than a distant memory. As far as AmEx is concerned, this is priceless. The travellers' cheques themselves don't generate interest, while the money paid for them is invested by AmEx and earning 6 per cent or more.

You don't have to, but you are expected to earn 150 Shopco club points during each collection period, each of which lasts about three months. The card encourages and glorifies loyalty, which is good for Shopco and makes the customer feel happy about himself or herself and comfortable that the store is a secure, reliable and friendly element in his or her life. Take out a card and, over the years, the information this little slip of plastic transmits in code to Shopco, via the till and the data-base, becomes the spy in your purse recording what you are doing with your life and drawing conclusions from your buying habits. It won't just tell the analysts in their rooms at Shopco HQ in Hertfordshire, that you own a pet, wear dentures or suffer from trapped wind. By applying sophisticated socio-demographic software to your lifestyle, and that of twenty million other customers, they will be able to determine the stage in your life that you – and others in your household – have reached. your lifestyle will bring influence to bear on all sorts of products sold through Shopco's three thousand stores. Your buying habits will be passed on to the manufacturers of your pet food, your denture cream and your electric kettle. From this,

Shopco will make assumptions about the size of your income, your hobbies and interests, your drinking habits, your attitude to healthy living, your sex life, your literacy level and your disposable income, and will determine your position in the socio-economic firmament according to the technicians at Shopco Megacorp HQ. They will know when you move house, when you go on holiday, when you are ill, when you have had a baby.

But that's OK. After all, they're only grocers and they're just in it for the money. Or are they? When you move house and change the address on your card, the odds are that you'll receive a little gift of handy vouchers tailor-made for a new householder, perhaps for cleaning products, along with a list of addresses and telephone numbers of local stores. The level of generosity will correlate to your status on the database. As far as discovering that a new baby has arrived, the number-crunchers can work that out from the way you change your shopping profile. Suddenly, disposable nappies and formula milk appear as regular purchases on your database. Perhaps they'll invite your to join their Toddler Club? It sounds rather charming, really, put like that. The retail industry now owns vast amounts of information like this about us. Under the guise of improving their performance and the service they provide for their customers, they have created knowledge banks that would be beyond price to all sorts of groups, including many that you would most certainly not want to share your personal details with. The problem here is that these are not bank details we're talking about. They are customer details collected by retailers. If a grocer sees the chance of profiting from a resource such as loyalty card data, he'll be tempted to take it. But who knows where that information might end up? American supermarkets voluntarily provided their loyalty card details to the FBI after

9/11. Fair enough, you may say, that was a real emergency. But it was also the thin end of a very thick wedge. It has made it easier to release data to politicians who you may not support and who you may not want to own your personal details. The customers on the supermarket databases were never told that information about them had been passed to the government. It was an invaluable aid to the federal authorities who were in the process of creating an intelligence formula that would help them to identify terrorist potential. In the aftermath of the atrocity, FBI agents studied loyalty card transactions of the hijackers as part of their attempt to create profiles of their shopping habits.

Much of the modern politician's armoury revolves around the identification of target groups, which is exactly what a loyalty club is trying to do. Recent reports published in Britain and the US suggest that the release of this data may be more routine than the retail industry would like us to believe. In the UK, the Conservative Party has developed "Voter Vault" while New Labour has a similar database called "Labour Contact". Voters are divided into distinct groups differentiated by socio-economic criteria such as the car they drive, their postcode and where and how many times they go on holiday. The data enable the parties to predict our voting intentions, which in turn helps them to decide on the message they will target us with. Direct contact with the electorate via personal mailshots and telephone campaigning is a technique that was refined in the US with stunning success by George Bush's campaign director, Karl Rove. He used 300,000 volunteers in a multi-level marketing campaign using precise data to target voters on a precinct-by-precinct basis. During the last three days of the campaign, volunteers for the Bush/Cheney team mailed 7.2 million voters. Much of the information they used came from loyalty card databases. A similar approach was taken by all three parties in the 2005 UK general election.

The Australian Lynton Crosby, who helped John Howard win four consecutive victories in Australia, used the Mosaic classification system developed by Experian, the Credit Rating and consumer data company, during the 2005 Conservative Party Campaign. The scheme divides the population into sixty-one categories and eleven groupings. The list of voters used by the Conservative and New Labour parties was based in part on the 2001 census and in part on the intelligence from consumer surveys and spending records taken from loyalty card databases.

Database analyst Joe Patel, writing in the *Atlanta Constitution*, said that grocery stores routinely sell and trade customer preference databases compiled from those ever-popular discount shopping cards. *Media Week* has stated that Tesco, Thomas Pink, MVC and New Look have all released their customer information for sale to other marketing companies. The Caspian Group, which campaigns against loyalty card schemes, says that card data are routinely used in British and American courts. Sales details can be stored together with film images of cardholders. Caspian claims that there has been a rise in cases of shoppers finding themselves in hot water because of mistakes made by analysts when studying the data. With so much information being collected and new uses being found for it every day, such problems are bound to happen and abuses will begin to creep into the system.

There have already been examples of analysts changing the software to allow illegal access. A woman in Milton Keynes was arrested and her house searched by police after she was filmed on a supermarket's CCTV system placing her own scarf in her handbag. The store security believed she had stolen the scarf, and then tracked her through her loyalty card details. While it is difficult, if not impossible, to eradicate all risk of incidents such as this involving any company with which you do business, you can reduce your participation in programmes where it is not mandatory to provide personal information. And as a reminder, even if you are using a "fake" identity with your local supermarket, as soon as you write a cheque or use a credit card, they can tie that information to your "fake" profile.

It's not the data that are the problem, it's the human beings who are in charge of them. You are dealing with an industry which tolerates concepts like "Wizmark", an 8.5cm screen that is placed in urinals and activated by the movement of liquid. The flowing movement triggers a display of flashing lights, accompanied by an advertising message. As far as retail marketing is concerned, anything goes.

The risks of privacy invasion have increased dramatically with the introduction of radio frequency identification (RFID) on a wide list of products. The system uses tiny computer chips, smaller than a grain of sand, to track goods at a distance. They're known as "spychips" and have been concealed in the packaging of many products – such as Gillette razors – that you might buy at any supermarket. Each chip is hooked up to an antenna that picks up electromagnetic energy beamed from a reader device. When it senses the energy, the chip responds by sending a unique identification number to the reader allowing the item to be identified. The "spychip" can transmit information from a couple of centimetres to as much as thirty metres away. The technology has been available since 1999, and all the major British retailers have been conducting feasibility tests on the system. Unless there is organized and vociferous consumer antagonism, they will eventually tag every manufactured item on Earth with the system as replacement for the barcode. Tesco, Procter and Gamble, Gillette and Wal-Mart have all experimented with it. Trials in the UK have been partly funded by the Home Office, a political marker that will doubtless be recalled at some future date when the retail industry is finally held to account.

At its most benign, the technology helps to track goods from the manufacturer to the warehouse and then to the store. It could help to recover lost orders or notify security staff when a product has been stolen. In the not-too-distant future, manufacturers of household goods could catch up and, for instance, create a technology that tells you how to roast the frozen duck you have just bought, and how to make a tasty sauce. Resistance to RFID is based on the protection of privacy. With a standard barcode, a product such as a can of Diet Coke has a universally identical product code. If the barcode was replaced by RFID, every can would have a unique ID number. This could be linked to the customer who bought it because he or she could be identified when a credit or loyalty card is scanned at the till. So, if you go to Shopco, and buy a bottle of Head & Shoulders that is tagged with RFID, pay for it with a Visa card and claim your points on your loyalty card, you will be irrevocably linked with that shampoo (and the fact that you have dandruff). The retailers put the case that the identifiable range of the tag is very short. This is not true, because the chips can be read at a distance with more sophisticated reading equipment. Not only that, they also can be read in your purse or wallet and through your clothes without your knowledge. All that is required is the right sort of reader device. It means that when you are linked to a tagged product, a stranger can train a covert reader device on you to identify the contents of your bag or briefcase, and what you keep in your pockets, without your knowledge.

When it becomes widely used in the UK, the technology will allow the system to track your movements twenty-four hours a day. If the retail industry gets its way, there will be RFID tags and readers everywhere. They will be hidden beneath the floor, in aircraft, shops, refrigerators, hotels. Not only will we lose our privacy, we will be constantly bombarded with electromagnetic energy. The technology has developed fast and it is now possible to "print" spychips. This means that a full stop on a printed page or on a piece of plastic could be used to track you. The antennae can also be printed, thus making spychips virtually invisible.

The technology, originally developed in Japan, is currently downplayed by retailers as little more than "radio barcodes". It has been adopted as an alternative to normal barcodes, which are not considered secure and are increasingly subject to fraud. The retail trade's probable shift to RFID has alarmed pressure groups who are aware that the tags can be widely read by readers outside the stores. Consumer and civil rights groups have been trying to force a worldwide a ban on, for instance, Shopco's stores because they have been expanding trials of the system. They believe that RFID tags should be confined inside the warehouse and logistics chain and not permitted to pollute the info-space with anti-privacy pollution beyond the checkout. According to the Caspian Group, RFID is too electronically simple to allow for the incorporation of encryption technology that might provide some safeguards. To make matters worse, spychips cannot be "killed" (cancelled) at the checkout, and so continue to operate indefinitely. Shopco have expanded their twelve-month trial from two stores to ten and have ordered four thousand RFID readers and sixteen thousand antennae from Fire and Security's ADT Security Services. Marks and Spencer carried out a trial at six of their stores in 2004. During the trial,

M&S customers were not warned that they were buying tagged goods.

The only likely drawbacks to RFID tags will be the cost and the law. The technology is expensive, currently holding steady at slightly above fifteen pence each. This puts a fairly hefty premium on, for example, a can of Diet Coke, and the cost is likely to remain high for the immediate future. It is also possible that RFID tags contravene the UK Data Protection Act and European human rights legislation. It is certain that these schemes will be tested in court, both in the US and in Europe. In Germany, the Metro Supermarket chain incorporated RFID into their loyalty cards and justified what they had done by arguing that it allowed them check the age of shoppers who wanted to view adult DVD trailers. The data about the shopper were stored in a database linked by wireless LAN communications to an RFID reader in the DVD section of the store. Metro eventually abandoned the trial following protests by customers. "We'll go back to using barcodes," they said. However, they went on to comment that none of the other areas where Metro is using RFID technology will be affected by this decision. "We are committed to using RFID in the area of supply chain management." The store now requires most of its suppliers to attach smart tags to their pallets and transport packages. Target, the US retailer, placed a similar requirement on their US suppliers from 2005. It is only a matter of time before similar systems are used in Britain.

RFID technology is in its infancy but will soon become a regular part of our lives. It is most widely accepted in the US where it is used in the gambling industry. There tags are embedded in gambling chips as a means of reducing fraud and keeping an eye on the big players. British casinos have examined the system but have so far declined to use it, citing cost and limited need (it would be like taking a sledgehammer to crack a nut, they say). Students in colleges throughout America are monitored by means of the cards they carry, in which the tag is embedded. When they arrive at school in the morning, the RFID activates a screen to record their arrival and display their photograph. It does away with the older manual methods of maintaining a student's attendance record. Today, instead of checking off students' names on a clipboard, the system is computerized. Schools and colleges that use it say they do so in order to promote better security, improved timekeeping and greater efficiency. Ten local education authorities in the UK are currently testing a similar idea. It's the same system used to tag British offenders confined to house arrest or curfew, prisoners in penal institutions in Texas, and Iraqi prisoners of war. IBM has announced that it plans to include electronic tags in credit cards and cheque books.

Since the easing of rabies quarantine regulations for European pets, animals can be inoculated and the treatment recorded on an electronic chip implanted in the neck of the animal. Many thousands of British pets are tagged in this way and the chip also helps animal welfare officers to track and identify abandoned animals. It has become common, and in some places, fashionable for Americans to have tags implanted into their own bodies. Companies using the technology in Florida already advertise the simple operation and sell the technology on the basis that parents and childcare workers can keep an eye on their children in their care using it. A security company called Metrorisk embedded tags called VeriChips into the Attorney General of Mexico and dozens of his colleagues and staff during 2004. The chip allows them to gain quick access to secure buildings and courtrooms without hand-held identity cards. It is true that when it comes to personal enhancement,

Americans tend to be less inhibited than other nationalities, who might draw the line at having identity chips implanted into their bodies as a time- and labour-saving device. The technology also exists in Britain. We can be tagged privately by cosmetic surgeons in Harley Street. However, this tends to be one practice that the British keep to themselves.

The applications for tracking have the potential to strike a mortal blow for civil liberties. The UK-based civil rights group Liberty says control of the system should not be left up to industry, security companies, or private lawyers and accountants, pointing out that the government has yet to announce any plans to regulate the information produced by RFID. The technology is extremely adaptable. The Oyster travelcard used on the London underground has been using the technology for over two years. The Oyster card carries the owner's name and address and registers every time it is swiped at the beginning and end of a journey. According to Transport for London, the data will be kept "for some time". If you pay for your travel with a credit or debit card, as many people do, your journeys around London are recorded with pinpoint accuracy. All British and European cars will be fitted with tracking devices from 2005, and you can already buy mobile phones with tracking tags attached. The European Central Bank is planning to embed tags in all Euro banknotes by the end of 2005, and the Bank of America is studying a chip manufactured by the Japanese company Hitachi with a view to tagging US banknotes.

Thirty years ago, as well as making that prediction about computer processing power doubling every twelve months, the founder of Intel, Gordon Moore, said that any device or system that uses microchips will very quickly become smaller, more mobile, more efficient and less costly. Moore's prediction applies equally to the internet which is built on systems that break up data into "packets", or fragments, distribute them to the correct destinations and reforms them in a nanosecond. The system, known as TCP/IP has been able to absorb a wide range of technology in addition to internet communications, including the World Wide Web and the mobile phone service. It will not be long before our telephones, laptops, pagers, in fact all our communication devices, will come together to create the most massive surveillance system ever conceived. The days of cash transactions are coming to an end and every purchase will become a datapoint recorded on a hard disk and associated directly with the personal details of the individual involved. The record will remain until the disk is destroyed.

Loyalty cards and tracking devices will give private businesses more personal information about ordinary men and women than even the most tyrannical police state currently possesses. Are the benefits we receive from this type of data-mining and technology worth the risk? The retail industry and the manufacturers of RFID systems have given assurances that seeking information about purchasing patterns is a worthy procedure that benefits everyone, and that it is nothing to do with monitoring individual members of the general public. But surely we should be able to opt out of schemes that we are concerned about? What sort of protection exists for the information that these organizations have collected about us? Movements recorded on loyalty cards have already been used as evidence in court cases. Few of us approach retailers to express our concerns about confidentiality and the private information they gather about us. RFID technology will be put in place whatever we do about it. Loyalty cards have become part of everyday life. The only safeguard we have is to throw away our loyalty cards and pay in cash.

Chapter Three: We've Got Your Number – And Your Name Too

Cheap, quick credit comes easy today. You can raise a mortgage simply by picking up the phone. They don't need to know much about you, just your name and address, "Do you own your own home, Sir?" and they'll give you a "Yes" or "No" in a trice. In a matter of a few moments they can flag up your credit rating by accessing one of a dozen massive national databases belonging to companies such as Experian or Equifax. Loan companies and building societies have contracts with all sorts of credit rating companies and use them remorselessly to get an opinion on every request. It's when it goes wrong that your difficulties start. Data companies mine personal financial information, put it on their databases and sell it. They know every time you miss a hire purchase repayment. The system is not always accurate because the data can sometimes come from questionable sources, or mistakes can be made. But you'll be lucky to get it corrected quickly because the credit rating people don't want to take any chances. They like to keep their lists just as they are. They don't want to run the risk of approving a borrower who subsequently defaults.

Dozens of companies sell personal information. No self-respecting lender will risk his money unless he's been in touch with one of the many credit rating agencies that has been collecting credit information on you throughout your adult life. He has to justify the finance to his shareholders or his boss, after all. At its simplest level, every adult has a comprehensive file that lists everything you have done that might have a bearing on your suitability as a borrower. The information on the file is bought or acquired through public records such as court reports, social security, the Land Registry and private records including any defaults on credit cards, bank loans or hire purchase repayments. The profile is recorded on a database and then sold on to subscribers – or anyone who needs the information and is prepared to pay for it.

Credit ratings are used by the police and security agencies to build up personal profiles during investigations. Some data is more valuable that others. It might be difficult to acquire, for example, or relate to an individual or group whose history is regarded as uniquely important to others. In Britain, under the Data Protection Act, the file must be shown on demand to the subject to whom it relates. But even then the company is allowed to make a charge for sending you details of your own record.

Experian is one of the biggest credit rating companies in Britain. It will tell the potential lender if a borrower has ever been declared bankrupt, has had to come to a voluntary arrangement with his creditors, bounced a cheque, defaulted on a credit payment of any sort, or been convicted of fraud. It will occasionally offer little snippets of information that may be useful to lenders, such as the subject's social security or driving licence number, how many motoring convictions he has had, and whether he has habitually changed his credit card supplier in order to get a lower rate. The bank or credit supplier that subscribes to the service pays a fee for the data and tends to rely on it absolutely. Credit is very big business and those who lend tend to be hard nosed about what they do. No possibility of an exception to the rules is considered.

Credit-related data is not the only intelligence available in the information market. Prospective employee profiles are routinely bought by head hunters and public bodies, including local education authorities and police forces. In the UK, where the "predatory paedophile" has become the modern bogeyman, there are now very stringent rules and regulations governing who is and who is not acceptable for employment in situations involving children. All teachers and education workers have their employment and other records minutely scrutinized before being cleared for work. Even golf professionals, swimming instructors and scout leaders must be beyond reproach if they are to be permitted to teach children. It is the responsibility of the employer to ensure that all members of staff have been cleared of suspicion before they start work.

The information peddlers are routinely commissioned to provide basic information. If this information is wrong, it can blight the lives of the individuals concerned. If the person who has been wronged wants to take the matter to court, his or her only option is to use the civil law of defamation – for which, in Britain, legal aid is rarely provided. He or she might also turn to the Human Rights Act, or the European Court, but wherever they look for redress, it will be a long and grinding legal process. In the United States there are laws to protect victims of inaccurate information. The most notable is the Fair Credit Reporting Act (1970), which regulates access to the profile and the right to correct errors on certain lists of personal data, but not on others.

Unfortunately, credit rating agencies and other companies that market personal information are notorious for providing inaccurate data. There are two main reasons for this: either they were given bad information in the first place, or they were given correct information but entered it inaccurately. While the Data Protection and Freedom of Information Acts in the UK ensure access, they do not necessarily guarantee that the material contained in the database will be speedily updated or corrected when it is proved to be wrong. It is a slack and often arrogant industry in its attitude to civil liberties. Instances in which members of the public have discovered that they have been classified, wrongly, as dishonest and that reports on their character and activities have been assigned to the wrong person, or are simply malicious, are commonplace.

Many elderly people are placed in embarrassing situations by the data agencies. Credit card companies often withdraw approval of transactions simply because the user has not taken advantage of his or her card for a while. Credit is then automatically refused at the point of purchase, with all the usual accompanying unpleasantness. There are many situations in which an individual's credit rating can be damaged through no fault of his. A typical example is the bank that is in dispute with one of its customers over an unpaid loan. The customer may genuinely believe that he or she is in the right. The bank decides, arbitrarily, to refer the dispute to a collection agency to deal with, and to pass information to the credit agencies such as Experian and Equifax. The customer may continue to dispute the debt vigorously, and so the first collection agency sells the "debt" on to another, more ruthless company. The "debtor", fed up with the constant harassment and simply wanting to get the problem off his back, decides to pays the second collection agency. However, the customer's bank now has the loan marked down as a default and refuses to change its database on the grounds that it has no record of the debt ever having been paid. The default is now irrevocable and remains on the debtor's credit record forever. Such debts are routinely sold to outside finance companies.

The information trade is multinational and the biggest companies – Equifax, LexisNexis and ChoicePoint – operate throughout the world. They are known as commercial data brokers and are huge, technically sophisticated businesses with millions of subscribers and billions of names on their databases. They also acquire information from databases all over the world. The personal information they hold is not necessarily confined to credit-worthiness and character references for employers, either. Not only do they sell information to industry and commerce, they also provide it to government departments and the police,

LexisNexis recently admitted that personal data on 310,000 US citizens may have been stolen in a security breach in early 2005. When first taxed with the problem, the company claimed the security breach involved just a few of their many databases and only affected 32,000 people – about 10 per cent of the true number. LexisNexis said that its databases had been fraudulently breached at least fifty-nine times using stolen passwords, allowing access to addresses, social security numbers, and other sensitive information. This was the latest in a long line of determined and successful attempts to hack into personal intelligence that has affected hundreds of thousands of members of the public in North America and Europe.

In testimony given before Congress, privacy and civil rights groups, such as the Electronic Privacy Information Centre (EPIC), have demanded much stricter regulation of data brokers, arguing that there is too much secrecy and little accountability in their business practices. Complaints against Experian and other credit reporting agencies have been many and varied. Privacy has become a sensitive issue in a world in which everything we do is recorded and registered on a database. Strict regulation of the industry is long overdue. ConsumerInfo.com, a subsidiary and supplier of data to agencies including Experian, Equifax and TransUnion was alleged to have violated American law by advertising a "free" credit report which, as soon as the order is made, locks the consumer into a high cost, long term subscription service without adequate notice of the terms, including get-out procedures. The company was also accused of drumming up business by raising fears of inaccuracies in reports and so driving consumers to request copies of the reports or monitoring service via its website.

The action against ConsumerInfo.com was brought by EPIC, which pointed out the absurdity of the situation in which a credit rating agency advertises a subsidiary company through which you pay to check up on its parent company, as well as other agencies to whom it sold data. EPIC took the action as a way of demanding tight regulation of all credit reporting agencies and to force them to provide credit monitoring services to consumers without charge. In the UK, you have to pay £3 to see a copy of your file. The ConsumerInfo.com advertising message pointed out that somewhere in the data marketing industry, there could be a company selling inaccurate information about you. The problem was that it could be the advertiser itself. This was Kafka at his best.

But it gets worse. When consumers agree to co-operate with a credit service monitoring subscription agency, they are required to provide personal information to validate their identity. The credit provider is allowed to share this information with all affiliates of the agency. The consequence is that most consumers who want to protect their privacy unwittingly relinquish all rights to it. This means that consumers seeking subscription services to credit rating companies to obtain some control over their information, privacy protection and credit accuracy, actually impede all those outcomes. Marketing practices by credit reporting agencies that exploit consumer fear of inaccurate credit reports are obviously questionable.

Simon Davies, director of the UK branch of Privacy International, is an expert on the growth of data marketing companies and has long experience of the problems that arise. Privacy International and its associate group, EPIC, have been involved in numerous skirmishes with companies like ChoicePoint, whose growth, particularly since September 11, 2001, has been spectacular.

ChoicePoint, based in Georgia, USA, sells information to insurance businesses, government agencies and the marketing industry, among others. According to its quarterly statement, filed at the Security and Exchange Commission, ChoicePoint sells: "claims history data, motor vehicle records, police records, credit information and modeling services ... employment background screenings and drug testing administration services, public record searches, vital record services, credential verification, due diligence information, Uniform Commercial Code searches and filings, DNA identification services, authentication services and people and shareholder locator information searches ... print fulfilment, teleservices, database and campaign management services..."

Since its spin-off from Equifax in 1997, the company has steadily accumulated a large share of the commercial data broker market by acquiring thirty-eight other businesses, and is now one of the biggest players in the game. These acquisitions include major data retention organizations such as Pinkertons inc, National Data Retrieval inc, CITI Network, Bode Technology, Accident Report Services and many more. The *Wall*

Street Journal has reported that ChoicePoint recently provided personal information to thirty-five or more government agencies, and the company also has several multi-million dollar contracts to sell personal data to law enforcement groups.

The sort of information that ChoicePoint is selling to government agencies includes credit headers – the identifying information that appears at the top of a credit report. This includes the individual's name and address, spouse's name, previous address, phone number, social security number, and employer. It also provides what it calls, "Workplace solutions pre employment screening", which includes financial reports, education verification, reference verification, criminal record, if any, motoring and driving convictions, and verification of social security numbers and professional credentials. It also offers a service called "asset location", which is a profile of an individual's wealth. It will even provide the facility to engage in "wildcard searches", which present law enforcement agencies with comprehensive personal profiles in a matter of minutes, often using nothing more than a first name or partial address. SmartSearch is one ChoicePoint tool that allows just such broad "wildcard" searches. By feeding all the details known about an individual, such as name, age, likely city or region of residence, into the database, it can pinpoint the one person to whom all these criteria apply and thereby find out where he is living. As well as residential addresses, ChoicePoint has a list of all US and UK military personnel, and aircraft and boat owners, to help them track down a subject.

One of the ChoicePoint's most popular products is a sophisticated service called AutoTrackXP. This allows much more information to be added to an individual's personal profile, including a facility called "linkage services", which finds numerous connections between the subject and other personal data compiled nationwide from, for example, clients and tax offices. For example, AutoTrackXP can compile past addresses of the subject, and the names of other people who have used that person's address, in documentation such as driving licences.

It gives details of all types of licence owned by an individual, including driving, pilots' and firearms licenses. It lists employment details, business information, professional credentials, qualifications and affiliations, property ownership and transfer records, vehicle, boat and plane registrations, social security number, and public record information, including arrests, charges, court judgments and bankruptcies. The product will also supply complete phone directories and reverse directory services (finding out who owns a particular phone number).

ChoicePoint has developed a technique called "Soundex" queries, which can search for personal information based on the sound of a name, rather than its spelling. It will also supply information on the neighbours and family members of a suspect. In fact, it will build up a complete neighbourhood profile and give a picture of a man's social circle and how he spends his leisure time, how he goes to work, where he buys his groceries and where he drives his car.

It seems obvious that huge organizations like this, which collect and disseminate massive amounts of personal information, must be regulated as tightly as possible. Yet many of their products do not seem to be covered by existing US legislation. Some "personal dossier" products, such as ChoicePoint's AutoTrackXP report, are sold on the basis that they do not need to comply with the protections provided by the US Fair Credit Reporting Act. This law broadly regulates the compilation, use, and dissemination of what are called "consumer reports".

The Federal Trade Commission (FTC) is currently conducting an investigation into ChoicePoint and other commercial data brokers. The investigation was prompted, in part, by a complaint filed by civil rights organizations in December 2004. These organizations urged an investigation into the "personal dossier products" provided by data brokers including ChoicePoint. EPIC argues that such products constitute "consumer reports" under the terms of the Fair Credit Reporting Act. If so, both information seller and buyer would be subject to the Act's regulations. An important point at issue was whether businesses, private investigators and law enforcement agencies should be allowed access to data that had been distributed without the knowledge and permission of the subject concerned. EPIC and others believe that just because an individual agrees to provide personal data for the purposes of being granted credit, it does not follow that the information can be passed on to the police without that individual's knowledge. Most consumers are certainly against the idea of sharing personal information for purposes other than those for which it was gathered. In the UK, the Data Protection Act is designed to deal with this problem, although it has rarely been tested in the courts.

AutoTrackXP reports are similar in scope and in use to standard credit reports that are normally protected by the Act. EPIC claims that by selling them without the Act's protections, ChoicePoint is subverting the policy goals of federal information privacy law. According to EPIC, companies such as ChoicePoint and products like AutoTrackXP are turning the clock back to the days before legislation was introduced to provide protection for the subjects of data collection companies. In the past, such companies were unaccountable and consistently reported inaccurate, falsified, and irrelevant information on private individuals. Sometimes, in an industry as big as data collection, profiles could be deliberately falsified as a means of driving up the price of insurance or credit. In effect, individuals were falsely "blacklisted" as credit risks and so had to pay much more for their credit facility or insurance cover, usually from less reputable companies. Naturally, ChoicePoint dispute these allegations, and has called for a national debate on the topic.

Other issues taken up by the privacy campaigners in America are also relevant to the rise of commercial data brokers. One was highlighted in an article in the *Washington Post*, which claimed that ChoicePoint acts like an "intelligence agency" and that the data industry should be subject to new regulations because of the way personal information is being used. The *Post* article made the point that there is now a huge reliance on commercial data brokers for information upon which official planning can be based. Since 9/11 the use of personal data has grown in importance in the US and the UK. It is vital that the information used to create massive anti-terrorist data systems such as CAPPS11 is accurate and that the data sellers' practices are accountable to the public. ChoicePoint has around one hundred thousand clients, including contracts with seven thousand law enforcement agencies. This does not include its British and European clients.

Evidence given by EPIC to the Federal Trade Commission investigation included a transcript from the Politechbot.com mailing list. This concerned a private investigator who uses ChoicePoint and who had claimed that the company maintains an audit trail of clients who access personal information. EPIC's evidence points out that law enforcers are not subject to audit trails, and that there has not been a single instance where a commercial data broker has turned in a user for prosecution as a result of an audit showing prohibited use of the service.

EPIC also submitted a transcript of a television documentary called *Someone's Watching*, which was broadcast on December 18, 2004, on the Discovery Times Channel and viewed widely throughout the US. The broadcast shows two private investigators demonstrating just how simple it is to use a commercial data broker to access a stranger's social security number, employment details, and other information – without having any legal justification whatsoever.

Then, in February 2005, the data protection industry was rocked by one of the most astonishing admissions ever made. ChoicePoint was forced to announce that the company had sold personal information on at least 145,000 Americans, mainly in California, to a criminal ring engaged in identity theft. California police have since reported that criminals have used the ChoicePoint material to make unauthorized address changes relating to at least 750 individuals, and investigators believe the personal information of up to four hundred thousand people nation-wide may now have been compromised. Civil Liberties groups were outraged and demanded that the company should make available to those whose personal information was negligently disclosed the same information made available to the criminals. This was not only a matter of fairness and justice, they said, but also of critical public safety concern.

At a hearing before the California Senate Banking Committee, held in March 2005, data handling companies including ChoicePoint, LexisNexis, and Acxiom were severely criticized by Senator Jackie Speier, who chairs the committee. She wanted to know why it was that ChoicePoint's systems could be fooled so easily by relatively unsophisticated criminals, and why the company did not disclose the breach of data immediately it was discovered. In its reply, ChoicePoint apologized for selling personal information to criminals. It has now said that it will "discontinue the sale of information products that contain sensitive consumer data", including social security and driver's licence numbers, "except where there is a specific consumer-driven transaction or benefit", or where the products "support federal, state, or local government and criminal justice purposes".

To many, this seemed a very weak and guarded response, especially bearing in mind the consequences of their breach of security. Small businesses will still be able to buy ChoicePoint reports, the company said, but it appears that social security numbers will be censored. The company announced that it is working on a system to provide access to all its information products. However, individuals will still not be able to correct their 'public records' reports, even if patently incorrect. It confirmed that it would automatically remove social security numbers that appear in public records.

During the California hearing, the Senator asked about the data brokers' definition of "sensitive" information and whether that term included social security and driving licence numbers. When these same identifiers appear in public records, LexisNexis, for instance, does not consider them sensitive, and sells them without hesitation. Senator Speier said that she believed that to many people these details were "indeed extremely sensitive", and added that "the commercial data brokers" definition of 'sensitive' ... does not seem to reflect reality".

ChoicePoint has used fear in its advertising as a way of promoting its service. It claims, for instance, that the company prevents predatory paedophiles from attacking children and that many missing children have been found through the company's database. Senator Speier asked ChoicePoint what percentage of their actual business comprised finding lost children, but there was no answer to the question.

EPIC not only roundly condemned ChoicePoint's reforms as "inadequate" but also pointed out that they do not address the privacy implications of the commercial data broker industry as a whole. In particular, they do not bind the company's competitors, and so other commercial data brokers can continue to sell personal information such as social security details to whoever they choose.

EPIC went on to say that, "Neither [ChoicePoint's] minor changes to procedure nor revelations that there has been a series of breaches at major banks and universities has curbed a complex and often very shadowy marketplace of selling and re-selling personal data that is vulnerable to similar fraud."

ChoicePoint is apparently still planning to continue marketing its unregulated "public records" reports to small businesses, albeit with the social security and driver's licence numbers "truncated" – that is, abbreviated. But large businesses and law enforcement agencies will still be able to obtain full reports, complete with all "sensitive information" included in full. It is not clear how exactly the social security number will be "truncated". Some claim that it may be possible for small businesses and others to "reverse-engineer" the system, and obtain the full identifying number. The answer would surely be to eliminate the social security number from the report, rather than truncate it and risk that the user can piece the number together from several sources.

According to a report by the World Privacy Forum, ChoicePoint's public information reports have a "high error rate". In their sample, 90 per cent of the reports obtained by the Forum contained errors, many serious and others plain ridiculous, including one individual being assigned the wrong sex.

The Forum's analyst, Pam Dixon's initial findings are supported by frightening stories from others who have obtained their unregulated ChoicePoint reports. Richard Smith, a researcher, after reading his ChoicePoint report said that it "contained more misinformation than correct information". Elizabeth Rosen, a nurse living in California, one of the many victims of ChoicePoint's breach of privacy, found that five of the six pages of her report contained errors. For instance, her report mistakenly indicated that she was the officer of a business in Texas, that she maintained a private mail box at "Mailboxes Etc.," and that she owned businesses, including a delicatessen called "Zach's". The nurse also told the investigation of her frustration when the company refused to provide her with her full profile, and her long fight to see all the data that they had compiled on her. Asked at the hearing why ChoicePoint would not pass the file to the subject it concerned when requested, the company's representative failed to answer the question.

ChoicePoint now says that, in future, individuals will have "access" but not "correction rights" with respect to unregulated public information reports. ChoicePoint claims that it cannot correct the reports because the information comes from public records. However, a major problem with this excuse is that ChoicePoint has been guilty of mixing up public record information relating to different individuals. For example, Deborah Pierce, who managed to obtain her "National Comprehensive Report" from ChoicePoint, discovered that the dossier falsely described her as having a "possible Texas criminal history". That someone on ChoicePoint's database has a criminal record may indeed be accurate – but that record does not pertain to Deborah Pierce.

According to Simon Davies of Privacy International, in London, there is nothing to bind ChoicePoint to its promise to maintain its reformed policies. In recent years, many large companies including eBay.com, Amazon.com, drkoop.com, and yahoo.com have been found to have changed users' privacy settings or altered privacy policies to the detriment of users. Legally, ChoicePoint is in a good position to renege on its promises, as it does not acknowledge a direct relationship with consumers that could be the basis of a legal action. To ChoicePoint, its "consumers" are the businesses that buy data from the company, not the subjects of its personal reports.

ChoicePoint has issued a press release in which it states that it reserves the right to sell "sensitive" personal information to businesses in many different ways. The release states that sensitive information will be sold to, "Support consumer-driven transactions where the data is needed to complete or maintain relationships ... to provide authentication or fraud prevention tools to large, accredited corporate customers where consumers have existing relationships ... to assist Federal, state and local government and criminal justice agencies in their important missions." But what exactly are "consumer-driven transactions" and when is data "needed to complete or maintain relationships"? These seem little more than the frantic jottings of a dazed PR person who suddenly found himself in the media firing line.

ChoicePoint is in the happy position of being able to decide for itself what a "consumer benefit" is. In the past, the company has attempted to explain just what this term might mean. The company said it would resist attempts to delete any date contained in their reports because, "We feel that removing information from these products would render them less useful for important business purposes, many of which ultimately benefit consumers." ChoicePoint's idea of what benefits consumers differs from what consumers think benefits them.

The ChoicePoint policy allows the company to sell reports in full for anti-fraud purposes. While in theory this policy seems praiseworthy and sensible, almost any transaction can have some fraud risk. If this policy is maintained, it will allow the company to continue to sell personal data on individuals, even when the fraud risk is minimal or used as an excuse to collect information for some other purpose.

During the California hearing, ChoicePoint pulled back the curtain a little way and revealed the breakdown of its core business. It said that about 5 per cent of its business is "the distribution of data to support local and federal law enforcement agencies in pursuit of their investigations", and 6 per cent of its business "supports law firms, financial institutions and general business to mitigate risk through data and authentication including litigation support and providing information needed to collect lawful debts". The final 20 per cent of the business is the selling of software and technology services that do not include the distribution of personally identifiable information.

In policy debates, ChoicePoint does not always specify whether it is discussing its regulated or unregulated reports, thus confusing the public and lawmakers alike. Approximately 60 per cent of ChoicePoint's business is driven by "consumer-initiated transactions", most of which are regulated by the FCRA. Such transactions include pre-employment screening and insurance underwriting services, tenant screening, organizing the delivery of vital records to consumers, and filings for Title Insurance. Nearly 9 per cent of ChoicePoint's business is related to Marketing Services, none of which involve distributing person information, but which, even so, are regulated by state and federal "do not mail" and "do not call" legislation.

The fact that ChoicePoint's proposed policy "reforms" will not limit the sale of personal information to federal, state and local law enforcement agencies, nor the UK police, immigration and tax departments that access their data, must be a major concern to everyone who comes within their orbit. US civil liberty groups say that the legislature should approach the problems of the commercial data broker primarily as a privacy rather than a security issue. Even if personal information is being handled in a secure way, a major problem is that the company provides this personal information to a wide variety of organizations without the individuals concerned having any rights at all.

This is the future of the information market. There is a growing thirst for personal knowledge throughout America, Britain and the rest of Europe. What is missing, is the regulation and legislation to go with it. We are all being recorded all the time and the records are being sold. When we eventually begin to express our concern at our loss of privacy, it might be too late.

Chapter Four: Come in Number 15788659/54377...

Most of us believe that we are entitled to assume that all the data and information held about us by the state is secure and that the forms we fill in for the Inland Revenue and the Department of Pensions are kept between ourselves and our tax inspector. The notes taken about our health history, we have always believed, having been written down laboriously by our GP will remain with the authorities concerned and go no further. This is also what we believe will happen with the records kept by agencies such as Customs and Excise. We naturally feel the same way about the information on our children held by the Local Education Authorities, the Police DNA Database, The Criminal Records Office, the Police Facial Recognition database, and many more beside. The DVLA holds massive amounts of information about us and the vehicles we drive and it publishes endless analyses and learned papers on our driving habits. In fact most of our contact with the state is recorded and taken down, and may be used in evidence against us.

Every day of our lives we are touched by the state. We scatter information about ourselves to a variety of national agencies. Every visit to the doctor is registered on the NHS database, where the history of our health is charted throughout our lives and is available to the Secretary of State and thence on to whoever he or she decides can view it. Changes of address are registered with the Inland Revenue, the DVLA, and the Department of Social Security, and our wealth or lack of it is common knowledge to the banks, credit rating companies and the pensions agency. The Police National Computer and the Crown Prosecution Service databases have between them a complete, if not necessarily accurate, record of our criminal history. The National DNA database now has two million British citizens registered on its files, and the number is growing fast. The Telecom and mobile phone companies have massive amounts of knowledge about every adult in the UK. Every time you use a mobile, your exact location is logged, as is the destination of the call. The public utilities between them have enormous amounts of information about our daily habits. Now that water is metered in many parts of the UK, the water companies can even tell whether or not you regularly visit the lavatory during the *Money Programme*.

The Inland Revenue is still grappling with the difficulties of amassing a massive database on which every tax payer in the country will be registered and cross-referenced. The current estimate is that it will cost £30 billion when complete, although software difficulties have dogged the scheme and it is probable that the final cost will be considerably higher. The recent merger between the Inland Revenue (IR) and Customs and Excise has potentially created a much more powerful tax collection unit that will be able to provide a comprehensive overview of our declarations and cast up anomalies. Like most databases, however, its effectiveness will depend on the accuracy of the input and the ability of the staff to use it. While the data may well be recorded in detail, the Inland Revenue will always be forced to rely on forms and brown envelopes and it cannot expect all tax submissions to be accurate. IR does not only collect tax, it habitually forces employers to deduct repayments of student loans from their employees' salaries, thereby forcing businesses to become debt collectors as well as tax collectors on behalf of the Government. The Pensions Office, also now part of the Inland Revenue, has a separate database that lists our National Insurance contributions, employment records and financial history since the age of sixteen. The amount of information given to the Inland Revenue and recorded against us can also be cross-referenced against our bank and savings details and will be available to investigative agencies such as the Serious Fraud Office and the IR tax collection department in Worthing. They do not rely entirely on what they learn in this way, of course. They also employ officials who spend their careers investigating taxpayers and trawling through their careers looking for fraudulent or inaccurate returns.

In 2004, the National Health Service announced the launch of its programme to develop a computerized database. Contracts for the project, run by NHS IT, were originally worth £6.2 billion. Naturally, the project was soon running over budget and the costs, as of 2005, were estimated at £31 billion. The project involves the transfer of years of handwritten notes from general practitioners' records to a national computer based in Manchester. The transfer of the information will be carried out mostly by privately employed IT specialists. According to Health Minister John Hutton, the Government was offering the public a choice about the level of security their record enjoyed. "Patients will be asked if they want their medical records to be included in the database, or whether they would prefer them to be removed from the system and secured in an electronic 'sealed envelope', which will restrict access except in a dire emergency." The management of the NHS IT project then qualified this superficially reassuring guarantee by pointing out that patients restricting access to their records in this way will run the risk of clinical staff making mistakes during emergencies. Preventing access to records will mean less information is readily available about known medical problems including allergic reactions.

The NHS database will be one of the most complex pieces of data mining ever attempted anywhere. Its security is vital to everyone in the UK who values the sanctity of their intimate private life. Yet it is in the hands of politicians and civil servants to ensure that not a single item of health information gets into the wrong hands. There will be all sorts of legislation and the promise of dire retribution for anyone found hacking into the data. The Government has said that the database has advantages for all of us because it ensures that the doctor who treats us has all the most current and accurate information about us. It will be more secure than the traditional paper system and it will not be part of the data registered for the identity card database. However, health professionals have many reservations about the scheme. The public health records of the British people would be a priceless resource to the insurance industry, to law enforcement agencies. The drugs and insurance industries are multinational and wealthy and the value of a nation's health records would be inestimable to them. "Safeguards" mean little because emergency medicine can be a chaotic process requiring clinical professionalism and speedy treatment, and so fast access to records would be the priority. It is likely that there will be many occasions in an emergency ward when the security of a database will, understandably, come low on the list of priorities. The old written system was far too cumbersome for unauthorized people to access easily in large numbers or in great depth. No such difficulty will hamper the hackers who want to get into the NHS database.

It would be impossible to protect data in a busy accident and emergency department where staff share a computer terminal. Harold Cayton, of the National Care Records Development Board, has said that the sharing of patient information should continue to be a matter between the patient and his or her doctor. The Board is planning to publish a "Care Record Guarantee" (which my doctor says won't be worth the paper it's written on!). The British Medical Association (BMA) has demanded stronger assurances and safeguards from the Government. Some GPs and doctor's surgeries have even refused to hand over records. The fact is that patients don't have the right to determine what is recorded about them by doctors and there is no GP or other professional body which is clearly responsible for protecting the information collected. It seems obvious to many that civil liberties will be in jeopardy.

The Driver and Vehicle Licensing Authority is part of the Department of Transport. It has been operating as a computerized database since 1980, and issues us with licences and processes our road taxes. It is the repository of our driving records and the history of the cars we have owned. The DVLA also notes the address of the owners of all vehicles, insurance cover, our motoring offences and punishments, driving bans, provisional licenses and driving tests, and the maintenance record of our cars. It constantly researches rates of car crime and sentencing, broken down into the sex and age of the offender, and retests after convictions of dangerous driving or driving under the influence of alcohol. It produces analysis of reoffending statistics, disqualifications and the survival of accident victims. It examines the effect of drugs on driving and advises the judiciary and magistrates on sentencing policy. DVLA is thus involved in the administration and the law concerning all drivers in Britain. Its database is comprehensive and is in constant use by police forces throughout the UK and overseas.

The database contains records of stolen cars that are downloaded to all police forces using numberplate recognition systems. The database is also routinely handed over to insurance companies and to the London Congestion Charge Scheme. The software for the DVLA system was installed by Capita, the Government IT sub-contractor that has out-sourced its database software development to India in order to exploit low-cost labour in the Asian sub-continent. Civil liberties organizations believe that this will make DVLA data widely available in the developing world. The authority has many decades' experience in data handling and claims that "the security of the information is tight". But not tight enough. There have been numerous examples of data being accessed illegally via the DVLA's vehicle licensing computer and the criminal records bureau. Saul Dickinson, an animal rights extremist employed by the DVLA, passed on the names, addresses and vehicle numbers of staff connected with a guinea pig farm in Staffordshire. The information was used in a campaign to terrorize families working at the farm. Dickinson was jailed for five years.

Awash with resources, the police forces of Britain are enthusiastically embracing the technological revolution. Testing for the Police DNA database has now been privatized and samples are taken from everyone who is arrested or involved in a crime in any way. There are now two million individuals entered into the database and this will expand rapidly as a result of changes in the law. Most people on the database will never have been convicted of a criminal offence, but under current rules their data will be kept on it for life. Samples are taken from cheek swabs, hairs and bodily fluids, and checked against samples found at crime scenes. The risk with DNA information is that it can be used to provide data that has nothing to do with criminal offences. For instance, it can reveal details of family relationships, including non-paternity, and reveal genetic tendencies to ill health that would be useful to the drug and insurance industries. Genewatch, a civil liberties group concerned with the uses of human genome information, believes that there should be an independent, transparent and accountable public body appointed to make decisions about the DNA database. Samples should be destroyed after use they believe; there must be an immediate ban on genetic research using the data; and the effectiveness of the DNA database in tackling crime should be analysed independently. The use of DNA evidence has already resulted in serious miscarriages of justice in the case of women accused of harming their babies. Genetic research has already been privatized. A project called UK Biobank plans to gather and analyse the genetic data from five hundred thousand volunteers for up to thirty years. Their objective will be to identify those genes linked to diseases. Of great interest to the life insurance business, no doubt.

The Police National Computer is a national database that lists convictions for "recordable" offences – that is, for which a prison sentence could be given. They must be removed from the database after ten years, or five years if the person concerned is issued only with a caution. Three or more convictions, and the record remains on the database for twenty years. There are, of course, exceptions, such as convictions for sexual offences, violence, child molestation or an unfitness to plead because of insanity. The PNC is instantly available for access by the nearly quarter of a million police officers in the UK. The database is constantly being expanded. A new facial recognition system is being assessed in town centres in Yorkshire, Strathclyde and several Midlands police forces. Facial recognition has been used extensively elsewhere and has not yet been successful. It involves the recording of biometric facial measurements. There are sixty separate identifiable parts of the face, which together form a unique portrait of an individual. Unfortunately, that is as far as it goes. A police identification photograph taken and digitally stored after an arrest is sharp and the subject is stationery. The face of a criminal in a shadowy town centre at night is another matter altogether. At the moment it looks to be an expensive and unsuccessful experiment. However, several million pounds of local police authority budget have already been spent and will have to be justified. Facial recognition technology has not yet been tested in the British courts, but who is to say that it won't be in the near future, and that it will not result in misidentification and miscarriage of justice?

Throughout the country, the police are working with local education authorities to bring an end to truancy. For the first time ever in the UK, problem children have been listed on computers in several parts of the country. When caught, persistent truants are likely to be given an Anti-Social Behaviour Order (an "ASBO"). In extreme cases, their parents can be – and have been – jailed. The storage of a child's details on a national database is a serious issue. Civil liberties organizations are concerned that yet another barrier has been brought down. The criminalization of children already exists in the US, where a five-year-old girl who was having a tantrum at her school in Florida, was handcuffed and taken away from school by police officers. Children have been imprisoned in Britain, but including them on an education authority database could be the beginning of a dangerous downward spiral. So far, even badly behaved kids will not be expected to carry ID cards, if and when they come in.

National identity cards are in use throughout the world. They vary in function and integrity, including health care and social security. Some are compulsory, others are not. Some use numbers to identify the holder, but most incorporate an electronic strip. The plastic card has taken the place of the identity "papers" because it is more difficult to forge and because the card manufacturers promote themselves well and can easily update the system on a regular basis, adding more information about the holder and his or her family as it becomes available. Around one hundred countries have compulsory ID cards. The United States, United Kingdom, Canada, Australia, and New Zealand, however, do not. The Australian and New Zealand public rejected the proposal for peacetime ID cards outright after holding referenda. Canada abandoned its proposal for a biometric ID card early in 2004. And even following the 9/11 attack, vociferous proposals for an identity card were firmly rejected by the US Congress.

The ID card is usually established in a country because of race, politics, religion or security. The former British Home Secretary David Blunkett announced plans for a national "Entitlement" card in October 2001, immediately after the Twin Towers tragedy. His stated reason was to tighten up anti-terrorist measures by making it harder for illegal immigrants to operate in the UK, and to counteract benefit fraud. The Entitlement Card was to be a compulsory ID card in all but name. Every citizen who applied for it would have to pay £75 and provide fifty pieces of information about themselves. There was immediate opposition to the idea. Former Home Office Minister Mike O'Brian said that, "Ministers have already recognized that our aim is to seek to protect freedom and democracy. Every time we are forced to undermine these values, terrorists will claim it as a victory." It was also said, with justification, that even if there had been ID cards in the US, they would have done nothing to stop 9/11.

Blunkett backed down over the proposal but attempted to reintroduce the card in February 2002. After a barrage of criticism from the House of Lords, he removed the weasel word, "entitlement" and described it as what it was intended to be – an identity card. He conceded that it would not be compulsory to carry the card at all times. However, it would be required to get health care and social security. Job-seekers would have to produce it when applying for work and other "entitlements". The Conservative Party initially came out in support of the card and then changed its mind and opposed it. Those who criticized the plan were accused of being "soft" on terrorism, a political mortal sin. The Bill was withdrawn before the 2005 General Election was called as there was insufficient time for it to progress through Parliament.

Whether or not the card is ever imposed in Britain depends partly on events and partly on the introduction of changes to other identification documents, such as passports containing fingerprint information. It also depends on whether the public fully understands what they will have to do when they agree to apply for the ID card. Most people believe that it is just a simple piece of plastic, although it is actually a vast, complicated and far-reaching system that involves an unprecedented use of personal information.

Support for a national ID card is strong among some politicians, yet the advantages are by no means clear. What will actually happen if and when they are introduced? It is a straightforward Bill. Firstly there will be a National Identification Register, which imposes an obligation on the Home Secretary to create a Central Population Register containing details of every UK citizen over sixteen. Secondly, everyone will be allocated their own unique number which will be known as the your National Identity Registration Number (NIRN). This number will be the key enabling government agencies to access, and share, information about us all. Clause 5 says that we must submit to demands to supply biometric or other forms of physical identification, which might be a facial recognition photograph or simple prints of our index fingers, as used in the US Immigration system. We will have to buy and keep a plastic card which enables direct contact from the database. Clause 15 makes it a requirement to produce the card when we wish to take advantage of public services. The sixth component states that the "unique" number and the register will be used by a variety of agencies as their administrative basis.

There will be a "cross registration component" that requires all government agencies to notify each other about changes in our details. This permits the bringing together of all registration numbers such as National Insurance and National Health Service numbers. For instance, if we tell the Department of Social Security that we have changed our address, they are bound to inform the NHS, Police, and so on.

Clause 19 of the Bill allows for the disclosure of information from the Register, without the individual's consent, to, among other agencies, police organizations, the Security Services, the Inland Revenue and Customs and Excise, the Department for Work and Pensions and the Serious Organized Crime Group. The Bill will also establish a range of new crimes and offences which are designed to make sure that the public comply with the ID requirements.

Described in this way, it's not quite the cuddly bit of plastic we may have hoped for. The information the Government says it needs is detailed and intrusive. Perhaps the most alarming aspect of the draft Bill was that it contained no provision for

Parliament to decide what information will be stored on the database. This decision is to be left to the discretion of the Home Office, which will be able to increase the requirement for information whenever it chooses. The Home Office has said that it will want to know where we have lived in the past, including full addresses and postal codes, and will ask for "information about occasions on which recorded information has been provided to any person, including photograph, fingerprints, iris recognition, National Insurance number, passport number, driving licence and any other official document".

There are, however, serious civil liberty difficulties with identity theft in Britain and the United States, although the problem is less critical in Europe. Germans happily carry ID cards at all times and, like all members of the armed services in the UK, generally tolerate the requirement, having learned to live with the idea. However, their systems are considerably less intrusive than that proposed for the UK. Americans are forced to conduct their lives and operate their businesses electronically. They are constantly asked to prove that they are who they claim to be. In practical terms this has meant that private "data elements" are contained in software installed in thousands of computers. Passwords, social security numbers, maiden names, birth dates, zip codes and other pieces of unique data, are used as authentication. The problem is that these details are now easily available to hackers and, with the widespread use of Wireless LAN, if the data is not encrypted it is easily accessed by anyone nearby with the right equipment who wants to look into your computer. Identity fraud is big business in the US. In 2002, the FBI arrested three men who had stolen thirty thousand credit reports and were selling them for use in identity theft schemes. Hackers also managed to infiltrate a company that processes credit card transactions and stole ten million AmEx, Visa and

Mastercard numbers. The fact is that the cosy old concepts of personal identity no longer apply in the US and Britain.

The reason for the increase in this type of crime is that too much information about ourselves is available to the determined criminal. As we have seen so far, all day, every day, the credit agencies, insurance companies, banks, supermarkets and smartcard operators gather information about us. And then they sell it on. The watchers and gatherers, particularly the credit rating companies such as Experian in the UK, and database marketers like Acxiom in the US, oppose government regulation and claim that it would just make life more expensive and complicated. Credit is easy to get. An American company called Synovate, which tracks junk mail solicitations for credit cards, claim that there were around five billion offers mailed in the US last year.

There are now more than three billion Visa and Mastercard cards circulating in the world, generating vast profits for the companies that issue them. Thieves have become correspondingly more and more sophisticated in avoiding security measures. At the same time, the credit ratings agencies' records have become tainted by inaccuracies because much of the information generated by the credit card operators originates from computers rather than people. Most of today's banks have no cashiers, managers or branches, and data is spewed out without any recourse to checks of any sort. Human beings cost money, which the credit ratings agencies and credit companies are not keen to part with. Some people might still find it hard to understand why the ID card has become so politically sensitive and so demonized by libertarian groups. The reason is that the world is now awash with personal information and the general public is loath to sign up to anything that ties us down even more.

The introduction of a National Identity Card was announced once again in the Queen's Speech in November 2004 and the proposal immediately attracted criticism. David Blunkett, whose own private affair with the *Spectator* magazine publisher Kimberly Fortier had at the time become very public when information about it was released to the press, had already stated in a Commons Debate in July 2002, that "It is important that we do not pretend that an ID Card would be an overwhelming factor in combating international terrorism. I have not made such claims, including ruling out their substantial contribution to countering terrorism." However, in the summer of 2004, while the Queen's Speech was still being drawn up, he said publicly that, "An ID Card *would* make a significant contribution to tackling terrorism." How could the two statements have been made by the same politician? Identity theft of the sort the card was designed to counteract. Of course, it was a political statement made against a background of increasing hysteria over the possibility of terrorist attack on mainland Britain.

The Bill predicted that the card would be in operation from 2008. The arguments against it, and any other government that wants to establish an ID card, were that it irrevocably alters the relationship between the individual and the state, and alters it for the worse. It means that, effectively, we will all have to apply to the Government for permission to exist. Unless we can go about our lives without using public services, watching the BBC on television, going to hospital after an accident, qualifying for a state pension. The law and order mantra that, "The innocent have nothing to fear," is easily dismissed when you remember the lessons of the other British Government computerized schemes that have ended in disaster, like the Passport Agency, the Child Support Agency, the Criminal Records Bureau, in fact virtually every government computer-based initiative.

Wherever in the world it is introduced, the ID card will instantly create another layer of bureaucracy. When you take your child to school for the first time, or visit the doctor, or sign on as a member of a golf club, the card will have to be checked by a public service gatekeeper who will be able to access the details on your card. It will be required during major "events" like applying for a driving licence, bank account or passport, when your eye will be scanned and matched against the biometric on the card. We live in an age when we are already drowning in red tape and the card will introduce another thick and expensive layer. The Bill included provision for a heavy fine of up to £1,000 if you omit to tell the police that you have moved house. What happens if you forget? The bill also requires your friends and neighbours to give information about you.

The Government justified the card by stating that 35 per cent of terrorists use false identities. Well that means that 65 per cent do not. What good will the card be as a means of deterring Islamic terrorists, visiting for a bit of R & R? The ID card may well reduce benefit fraud, but in the grand scheme of things this amounts to considerably less money than it will take to finance the card and so cannot be regarded as value for money. The Government estimates come out at a minimum of £2 billion to set up the scheme and it is likely that, as time goes by, costs will rise. The Home Secretary has made many claims about how important the card would be, with the emphasis on safety, security, locking people up where necessary and keeping them under control. Among other claims were reassurances that it would put a stop to health tourism and that the card would be used to check who is and who is not entitled to treatment under the NHS. Michael Wilks, Chairman of the BMA Medical ethics committee, responded by asking, "What procedure would be required in the case of an emergency when the patient does not have a card in his pocket? What are the implications if people have infectious diseases, but don't have a card?"

It is difficult to understand why politicians are so keen to impose identity cards on the public in an age when everyone is registered in great detail elsewhere. Knowledge is power and the card is naturally attractive to a party that believes in the concept of "joined-up government". A single database on which our entire personal history is accessible at the swipe of a card may appear neat and efficient to a politician – and horrifyingly intrusive to the man on the street. But perhaps it's the name "identity card" that gets under the skin. Why would you have to prove that you exist to a government that you have elected? The truth is, in the UK at any rate, that the British Passport is about to become an identity card in all but name. The data accessed through the electronic strip in the new document will be supported by a fingerprint. The Passport will cost £70, as opposed to the £42 charged now, and it could rise to £85 if the Government is forced to incorporate its plans for an ID card into the passport. The photograph is already there. In 2006, a minimum of 600,000 first-time applicants will have to be interviewed at the Passport Office and the number of offices run by the Passport Agency will rise from seven to eighty. Staff will be increased by five hundred. Very few of us know precisely what will be contained in the passport electronic strip. According to the Home Office, the increase in data included in the electronic strip is required to combat increasingly sophisticated fraud. As the threat of identity fraud increases, countries around the world are increasing the security of their passports. The new passport database will be subject to the Data Protection Act, however, and, according to Simon Davies of Privacy International, the final decision on the data it includes is likely to depend on the fate of the identity card.

Perhaps the most important question is, in return for handing over so much power, do we trust those we vote in, to run an identity scheme honestly and efficiently? Can they guarantee that the knowledge will be secure? Do we believe that they will tell us the truth about why the card is needed? Will they record information about us on the database about which we will not be informed? How will we ensure incorrect data about us can be corrected?

If you are a British citizen, it seems that your name will appear on at least half a dozen state databases. The new passport and the ID card will both increase the list of facts the state will know about us. The police DNA and the huge NHS databases will identify us through our bodies, and our health (or lack of it). Our criminal records are where they always were, except that they are now available at the touch of a button. In view of the problem of children bunking off school and the fear of child molestation throughout the community, how long is it before every child in the country has to carry a card and is listed on some computer somewhere?

I think it's just a matter of time.

Chapter Five: Fun and Games

Surveillance companies habitually test their products in casinos because the opposition in the person of the gambling cheat is the toughest opposition they can find. There is only one way you can guarantee to make money in a casino and that is to cheat. You can never beat the odds. Casinos may occasionally lose a million or so to a visiting gambling mad billionaire, but they always get it back in the long run because they benefit from an advantage called the "House Edge," which means all games of chance run by the house have inbuilt odds loaded on the side of the casino and against the punter. A casino makes an average profit of between 17 and 18 per cent. The Gaming Act is very strict when it comes to the gambling industry in Britain. Inducements are frowned upon. The occasional free meal and a chauffeur driven car, perhaps a glass of champagne, are acceptable, but hookers, first class flights and hotel suites are verboten in Britain. Other countries, particularly in the Far East and Africa, are easier One of the most interesting aspects of gambling is the array of cheats the casinos have attracted over the years. Some of the greatest brains in the world have been applied to winning at cards, dice and roulette, because the only way you can win in the long run, is to break the rules. It's a battle between the watchers and the twisters.

The most concise description of how a casino works is given by Robert de Niro in the film, *Casino* in which he plays the director of a big, flash gambling hall in Las Vegas. "How does it work?" he is asked at the start of the film. He says, "First up, you got the dealer; then you got the inspector watching the dealer; then there's the pit boss watching the inspector; then there's a Floor Manager watching the pit boss. I'm sitting upstairs watching the Floor Manager...Then you've got the eye in the sky watching everyone."

As well as the odds, a casino has two other advantages. Firstly it has money to spend on protecting its house edge; that means being able to afford every surveillance system known to man, and having the resources to pay for the best security staff. Secondly, they've seen it all before and have a thorough knowledge, based on a century of experience, of every trick in the book. The big London casinos bring in experts to lecture their security staff on how they are being taken for a ride. Brilliant cardsmen like the American Richard Marcus, one of the world's greatest ever cheats, who toured the world winning huge amounts by elaborate sleight of hand, regularly gives private presentations in London. He studied the array of technical equipment he was up against, had nerves of steel and understood the psychology of the watchers sitting up above the gaming floors with their cameras.

You can't corrupt the camera. It's the only thing you can trust because it doesn't have a heart, or a brain, and anyway, it doesn't gamble. You certainly can't trust the staff. You have to accept that everything that can be done to get round the system has been done at least once, and will be tried again. Corrupting dealers and security men has been successfully attempted time after time, but the casino owners learn from their mistakes and they have systems to discourage staff corruption, which is why everyone is watched like a hawk. Many casinos make the dealers wear aprons, not because it will protect their clothes but because it will make it harder for them to pocket the chips. Sometimes staff are searched after their shift and in some states in the US, chips are embedded with trackers so the boss knows where the money has gone.

The neural systems programmed to pick up and highlight anomalies of behaviour were first tried out in Britain by Ladbrokes. The moves in a gambling situation are disciplined and predictable. For instance once the bets are closed, no one may touch the chips on a roulette table. The same applies to blackjack, craps and all the games. A neural system trained on the green baize will pick up and highlight a late bet or the removal of a wager before the dealer announces the result of the play. As soon as it happens, security staff are there and the player is stopped. Richard Marcus made the surveillance system an ally by discovering that certain combinations of coloured chips confused the cameras in artificial light. He used this to make a great deal of money. Some casino surveillance was set up to resist late bets. Marcus would place a bet and only move it if it hadn't won. He worked with a team of three which enabled him to discover instantly the winning number at roulette and remove his bet in the chaos which ensues on roulette tables when the bets are about to be paid.

Manufacturers of equipment have been bribed to alter the balance of the roulette wheel or load the dice. Cards are marked, computers and cameras smuggled onto the gaming floor to see where the house advantage lies, magnets are fixed to the roulette table. The desperate desire to get one back on the casino and to get something for nothing, seems to obsess many in the punting community and haunt the gambling industry. Counter measures are in place against all these attempts at cheating in the big casinos. The gaming floor is filmed and watched twenty-four hours a day, the tables are tested with the most sensitive levels, the wheels are constantly balanced and checked and the cards are delivered in armoured trucks and stored in a safe.

Gambling is a vice. When it's bad and the gremlins have really got you by the nuts, it's not just a desire to win, to become a billionaire with yachts and private jets and beautiful women. The act of placing a bet becomes a drug; for many people it's like sex; a short release of tension after a long and difficult build-up. For some, the attraction is the dreadful anticipation once you've committed your wager and have to endure that heart stopping, three minutes of breathless dread while you wait for the white ball to take to the groove and settle in its numbered slot; or the final turn of a dealer's card, while your hands sweat and your heart pounds as you count the numbers. For some, the result doesn't matter; it's the powerful emotion caused by the last dregs of the family fortune slipping through the fingers. The high they experience from the play, win or lose, comes after years of chaotic bets and searing jubilation and disappointment. For others it is a desire to win at all costs. And there is a steely determination among watchers to prevent it. Casino staff are never employed without a minute examination of their profile and most casinos employ companies like Lexis Nexis to provide detailed backgrounds for all their staff.

Other know that there are ways to beat the house. There are schools in America where mathematics graduates are coached in the art of counting at blackjack. All you need is a big brain, a powerful memory, patience and the ability to alter the odds against the house by knowing exactly what card is where in the dealer's stack. The problem is that there are six packs of cards in the stack. Nevertheless, counters have been around for a long time. They play blackjack to a standard unimaginable to most of us and are caught and banned when they get too greedy or the Pit Bosses and the watchers in the rooms above the gaming floor identify them from their patterns of play. Sometimes they work it out from the face recognition software on their CCTV systems. They can occasionally tell that someone down there who seems to be consistently winning has been warned off elsewhere.

Biometric facial recognition software is regularly employed by American gaming companies. Caesar's Palace in Las Vegas uses it and advertises the fact, and it has been experimented with by many British casino operators. It is a popular system in the States where the Government determination to use it as an anti-terrorism measure has stimulated investment in the technology. The head of security at a London casino in Curzon Street told me that in his opinion, facial recognition is more efficiently carried out by the staff. "We have receptionists with long memories and we have found that their decisions on whether or not to allow a player into the club are far more reliable than any technology. Punters who have been banned will come back wearing disguises and false identities. No camera system can get round that. We rely on gut instinct. I have been reliably informed that the Caesar's Palace Facial Recognition technology is chaotic. There are thousands of gamblers on the floor and when you get a match in the monitoring room, you have to get men down there to pick them up. It's not always easy and it is not reliable in my opinion."

The first thing you realize when you enter a casino is that you're being watched, and they want you to know that you're being watched. Cameras are everywhere, every move is recorded and the images are sharp and broadcast quality. Pit bosses and floor managers are everywhere: cold-eyed men standing around in neat suits watching the gaming and the players. The dealers are working the tables, doing their best to see the bets and make sure that no one is past-posting, pinching or dragging (altering a bet after the play has been called). All gaming requires some basic technology. For instance the roulette wheel is regularly checked and properly balanced so that, when it spins there is no possibility of a bias which might upset the odds. Card decks are designed to a fixed standard and the chips are impossible to duplicate. The moves are picked up if the casino uses neural technology or the pit boss notices what is happening. "But however good the technology, you still need people on the ground," says my man in Curzon Street. "The neural system is impressive and it alerts you straight away, but things move fast and you have to get to the source of the problem quickly. This is difficult in a busy, crowded casino, however good your communications are."

Of course, there are anomalies in the industry. For instance, in the UK, equipment used in provincial casinos is often inferior to the beautiful state of the art stuff you will find in Crockfords or Les Ambassadeurs. The smart London casinos use the best available equipment, solidly made and hard wearing with all the wooden parts beautifully carved and inlaid and the bearings and spindles engineered and assembled by craftsmen. At the other end of the market, in provincial cities with tighter margins, where the punters go to gamble and don't expect the luxuries found elsewhere, the standard of furnishing in the gaming floors often leaves much to be desired. In 2004, four men were banned from casinos in the English Midlands after successfully executing a "Fat Man" scam. The procedure was eventually picked up by the surveillance system, but, although the evidence was there, it took a long time to detect. It required a team of three people to play. A heavily-built man would appear with a large number of low denomination chips and settle down at the end of the roulette table as far away from the wheel as possible. Two associates, who the fat man never acknowledged, would start to play and would in fact be keeping a close eye on the pattern of numbers as the wheel was spun. They had previously noticed that the green baize roulette layout and wheel was fitted to a comparatively flimsy piece of wooden board and that someone of substantial weight would be able to alter the plane of the table, thereby slightly shifting the roulette wheel onto an angle which would alter its balance.

Over a period of hours, with the fat man resting his bulk onto the end of the table, he and his associates were able to detect a pattern which would shift the odds in their favour. Having established a technique and become satisfied that it works, it is important to the cheats that they do not become greedy. Betting patterns and wins and losses are relentlessly charted in casinos, however lowly they might be. If the gaming takes persistently go against the house edge, then something is wrong and the watchers start searching. The team of three moved around, found other casinos where the standard of gaming furniture construction was vulnerable to a heavy man. As they perfected their technique, they soon started to clean up. They were caught when a sharp eyed watcher in Leeds who realized from the surveillance cameras what they were up to, had a camera with a fibre-optic lens installed in a pillar close to the roulette table. Of course, there was little evidence, there rarely is, but the industry has a simple answer when they are certain that some of their punters are up to no good. They film them, ban them, write a description of the scam and circulate it with the name and photograph of everyone involved, throughout the industry.

The records of most gaming companies are meticulous. They have to be because they are not dealing with something and long term like the law of the land, they're dealing with shareholders' money and it really matters to them. Crockfords, for instance, keep detailed data of every dodgy punter banned from any casino anywhere in the world.

The security staff in the industry are uncompromising and highly qualified. The head man at Crockfords came to the company when he retired as a Chief Superintendent in the Metropolitan Police in charge of the Clubs and Vice Unit at Charing Cross Police Station. His deputy is his second in Command, a Chief Inspector who ran operations against clubs in the West End. The same standards don't necessarily apply throughout the industry. Some are more experienced than others. The watchers are experienced in the laws of gaming. They've been employed because they've seen it all before and will have put away some of the most able of swindlers during their careers in law enforcement.

Gambling is international. The high rollers travel across the world to play. They live a lavish life and look for games where others like them will be. They play cards – generally poker or blackjack – and want games where the stakes are unlimited and the people running it are discreet. The cheats are international as well because they have to find new countries where they are unknown and can start afresh. The gaming industry is growing fast with huge new casinos opening in Australia, South Africa and the Far East. The introduction of new technology means new difficulties for the industry. British and American casinos have been looking at RFID as a means of keeping track on chips and the misuse of casino equipment and money laundering, but so far they have resisted the temptation to invest in radio barcodes because of the high cost of the technology. Not so the Americans, who have installed every technological system known to man in their casinos, including trackers.

There have also been no inhibitions among the criminals who see potential in electronic devices as a means of discreetly transmitting information over short distances. Early in 2005, eight Thai punters were arrested in Poipet, a resort town in Cambodia, close to the Thai border and the city of Chiang Mai. They had been caught using an "electronic device" to win bets at blackjack in the Star Vegas casino. They had won 90 million Baht, (over £1.2 million) The security staff at the casino said that they had been embedding microchips in the game chips which enabled them to scan cards and transfer the data to a laptop computer in a room in the hotel. Associates would contact them using mobile phones and coded messages, giving them details of the cards.

The importance of the Eye in The Sky to the industry is difficult to measure because it acts as a deterrent. The American Richard Marcus survived for years on his roulette scam, in which he would place a bet on the column known as "the 19 through 36." It was never picked up by cameras because the bet was made as far away from the croupier as possible and as soon as the ball cracked into its slot, Marcus would rake the wager away if it contained a high numbered chip at the bottom of the pile, or leave it if it didn't. He called it "The Savannah" and planned to play a "Super Savannah" at The Horseshoe in Las Vegas towards the end of his career. The bet, if it was success-ful, would pay $1,050,000. He abandoned it because the odds on hitting any single number at roulette are 37 to 1 and he would have to lay a bet of $30,000 to win. He would remove the bet from the table by past posting the wager but might have to do it several times. He knew that if he was successful, they would start going through the surveillance film and he would be caught. So he retired, although you have to ask the questions "is he really retired?" and "is he really as good as he says he is?"

The use of RFID has taken the problem of identifying cheating in the gaming industry onto a new level but in Britain the industry has been slow to take it up because of cost. A group of four Albanians were picked up in the Ritz Casino in London in 2004, and were arrested by the Club's Office after a complaint fro the Ritz security staff. They had won between £2 and 3 million at roulette and were reported for using an adapted cell phone and laser technology to corrupt the smooth running of the roulette wheel. The police were unable to prove what, if anything, had happened. The mobile phone was taken to pieces and examined by experts at Nokia. The arrest was principally the result of intelligence from casinos in France and Italy where the Eastern Europeans had also cleaned up large sums of money. Certain that they had been conned, the Ritz had refused to pay up but the investigation ran out of steam when the police could produce no forensic evidence and it came down to simple suspicion, which tends not to count much in the hands of a good defence lawyer. After six months of inactivity and frustration, the gamblers were paid out. They have left the country, and will, no doubt be gambling successfully somewhere in the Far East.

Gambling attracts larger-than-life characters. To be any good, you need nerves of steel, a fast brain, an understanding of odds and an appreciation of technology, particularly today in the world of microchips and sophisticated surveillance. To be a great gambler you must have a determination to win and a monster ego. Donald Trump, who owns the Trump Towers in Atlantic City was determined to have the highest casino in America, which turned out to be impossible because his hotel had only forty eight floors. He had the lift redesigned so that floors two to nine are missing which means that he can claim that his casino is on the fifty fourth floor. It means a lot to him.

Detecting the use of "counting" at blackjack is done through computerized checking of gaming patterns. The schools where blackjack "counting" is taught move around from hotel to hotel, masquerading as courses in accountancy or book keeping. The fees are high at £15,000 each for a two-week course and most of the work has to be done by the student, as the instructor puts them through ten days of concentrated mathematical mind games and practical work. One well-known school operating in and around Las Vegas also teaches past-posting and holds courses in sleight of hand. A counter will concentrate on working out where the higher numbers are in a shoe of cards and will make one serious bet before retiring. According to a security officer I have talked to, he can only be detected by casino staff who recognize him from his past record, and from his style of play. There are some methods which cannot be picked up by surveillance, only by the mathematical calculations of the gaming pattern.

The anomaly of surveillance in casinos is that, unless it is a neural system, it is not permanently watched because there are too many cameras recording what is going on. CCTV records are usually only examined if there is a problem and the dealer believes that he is being taken for a ride. The blackjack past posting is probably the most skilful method and must be executed fast, but it will be used for as long as the game continues to be played in casinos. If it is noticed by the dealer, it will be quickly confirmed on the CCTV, so the trick is to ensure that the casino staff don't become suspicious. There are seven playing sections on the semicircular blackjack table. The dealer stands facing the players in the centre behind the semi-circle. The past posting is executed using a simple, rhythmic move. The player comes to the table as the dealer is sweeping up the cards after paying the last winning bets. He places three £5 red chips on the position to the dealer's extreme right. This means that, after the hand is finished, the player will have been the last to bet and the first to be paid on winning. He will also be the first to have his bet removed if he loses. As he sits down, he puts five black £50 chips on the green baize before him, and covers them with his right hand so that they remain hidden to everyone in the casino. Tucked between the thumb and index finger of the same hand are the two "move" chips. In his left hand pocket he has another two dozen red chips. He plays the cards with his left hand, scratching the green baize with them and as he stands up, slipping the cards under the red chips. Because he is playing the hand to the extreme right of the dealer, he will be turned away from the rest of the table as soon as the hand is over. The position on the right creates a more pronounced angle between the dealer's head and the betting circle.

The player who is "past-posting" will never split a hand because he doesn't want a situation where the original bet has to be matched, which would give the dealer another chance to look at his chips. The player has slipped his cards beneath the three red chips, the hand progresses legitimately and he loses. Using only his left hand, he takes three more chips from his pocket and places them precisely in position on the extreme left of betting circle, again by the dealers right hand. He keeps his right hand on the table. He wins the next hand with a pair of kings and the dealer and one or two of the other players go bust. The dealer turns over the player's cards and immediately pays out three red chips. As he turns to the next player's cards, the player retrieves the three original chips he had bet, while with his right hand, he lays in two black £50 chips with a red "capper" exactly where his original chips had been. In the same motion, he drops the three red chips into his left hand jacket pocket and with his right hand, he taps the dealer's hand and says, "sorry, you haven't paid me the right amount," and flips the two black and one red chips onto the table.

When the floor man arrives he will only see the £205 bet and the black back up chips on the table. I have watched this move performed on CCTV and was unable to tell that it was past-posting because it was carried out with relaxed skill and at great speed. It is a mixture of dexterity and psychology. The watchers had not picked it up until some weeks after it had happened. The player was unlucky and he's since been black-listed. It means that if he wants to gamble, he will have to go back to the US. Where he came from.

Craps is a dice game which uses two casino staff and hence which needs three cheaters. The table is more intimate than other games because the staff are close to the actions and watching closely. The shooter, a punter throwing the dice, rolls them. If he throws a seven or an eleven, he wins. If he throws two, three or twelve, he loses. Anything else rolled is called a "point," and the dice have to be rolled again before he throws a seven to win. If the seven came first, he loses and the dealer removes the losing chips. Most craps tables are heavily watched and filmed because of the chaotic action around the game.

The team of three who will stage the past-posting in a craps game are the Fixer, the Claimer and the Dick. The Fixer makes the bet. Say he lays down three red chips. When he wins, he makes the switch, removing the original three reds and replacing them with the "move chips," two purples with a red "capper." He does this two handed, picking up the original bet with his left hand and replacing it instantly and in precisely the same place, with his right. It must be done in a fluid but rapid movement. As soon as he has completed the move, he gives way to the Claimer, who puts a "back-up" line of purple chips in the "players rack" along the edge of the table. The two casino staff, the "croupier" who announces the result of the roll, and the "Boxman," a supervisor who is seated between dealers and whose job is to watch the action and make sure the correct winnings are paid, will not have seen the Claimer until he starts to protest that he has not been paid out enough. The reason this matters is that the Fixer has been making regular bets of £15 and if he were to suddenly reveal that he has decided to make a winning bet of £2,005, they will get suspicious. A new player doing it is easier to accept.

The London casino staff I discussed the problem with agreed that neural systems offer the only possible solution to past posting because they instantly isolate the incident. To the system, the movements around a gaming table are irrelevant unless all the cameras recording the action are obscured, a very difficult situation to achieve. The craps table is, in a similar way to Roulette, often very lively and even with two casino staff at the table, a switch can be made without anyone noticing. It is also by nature a fast game with a rhythm of its own. Any decision by the supervisor or the pit staff to refuse a bet will be difficult to make. It's easier to give yourself a reason for paying up and getting on with the game. The cheaters' worst mistake would be to be greedy and try it again.

The third member of the cheaters' team is the "Dick," whose job it is to make sure that no extra security are around and that the Pit Boss is not watching the game. Professional teams will develop a silent language of their own, the two men who have carried out the switch will keep their eye on the Dick until the last moment before the move is made. The Dick will use signs like a cough or a wink to call off the move. He is also there to help the Fixer and the Claimer to leave the casino in a hurry if necessary. The Dick has to keep his eyes on the attitude of the staff and gauge the atmosphere on the floor.

This is where the CCTV system becomes critical. Casinos are understandably sensitive about exits to the premises because they carry large amounts of money and apart from the shareholders, the customers would become concerned about any situation in which the heavies started barring the front door and manhandling the punters. The trouble with surveillance systems is that they cannot predict what is going to happen; they record, rather than instruct. State of the art neural surveillance can help the monitor make decisions about a chaotic situation, but things can happen very fast on the gaming floor of a casino, particularly if the punters concerned have an exit strategy. There will usually be only one entrance to the building. If the situation deteriorates, the team will do their best to run out through the front desk and onto the street where they can disperse and be comparatively safe. If he's caught and he knows what he's doing, a good, professional punter will keep his mouth shut until he is released or can call his lawyer. But if he gets away with it, the claimer, if he has the nerve, will stay and make another bet, placing his red and two purple chips on the table before just walking away without waiting to see if he has a winner. It will make the Boxman, who may realize that he's been taken for a mug, feel better about what has happened and forget about it.

On the other hand, it may not.

Chapter Six: Hear All, See All

In the eyes of the public, spies are glamorous creatures. We associate them with an exotic lifestyle, and envy them for the dedication with which they quietly and secretly go about their work, defending our national interests. But the intelligence community is a huge, unwieldy apparatus that infiltrates every corner of our society. MI5, officially known simply as "the security service", is in the forefront of the fight against terrorism in Britain and is in the process of opening a network of regional offices and recruiting a thousand new officers. MI5 is powerful, but it cannot be referred to as a secret police force because it has no power of arrest. It relies on, for example, the police and departments such as Customs and Excise to do that. Nevertheless, MI5 wields enormous power and can "bug and burgle" its way through society at will. Never before have our secret services had such power. And of course our own "spooks" are not the only intelligence operatives working in the country – foreign spies are also over here. The Americans gather communications intelligence, and the French keep an eye on "home-grown" terrorists – both ours and theirs. Spying has never been so multinational and so technologically sophisticated as it is now. Spies are at the sharp end of the covert state apparatus and they have access to all our secrets.

Anyone who was in America around September 11, 2001, will remember the palpable change that came over the country; a mixture of shock and fear. I was working at the University of Pittsburgh at the time. It seemed that, all of a sudden, the streets emptied and the clean air was being sucked out of the sunny late summer afternoon. As an Englishman, I was out of place, an outsider, someone who had no right to be there. The President and his staff had disappeared, spirited away by muscular, stern-faced men in dark blue fatigues and armoured cars. Bush was taken by a circuitous route to Omaha, Nebraska, where he was kept safe in the Offutt Airforce base, the head-quarters of the Strategic Command. This ultra-secure command centre was developed during the Cold War. In the event of a USSR missile attack, it was from here that the President would take control of what used to be referred to as the Strategic Air Command and wage nuclear war. The remainder of the Government was distributed to top-security bombproof facilities in Maryland, Pennsylvania, Virginia, West Virginia (in luxurious underground quarters close to Sam Snead's old golf club, The Greenbrier), and New England.

The rest of the nation was left to its fate, it seemed. I found myself at Pittsburgh airport where a huge queue had formed. It was filled with US nationals desperate to return to New York – or wherever else their home was located – and foreign nationals from everywhere, desperate just to get out. The queues were patrolled by giant men and stony-faced women, tasked to deal summarily with disorder. The people stayed motionless for hours, silent, dispirited and frightened, exposed for the first time to the horror of an attack on US soil. The passengers were finally allowed to disperse to their destinations when it became clear that, in spite of the terrorist assault, air travel had to continue somehow and the country was beginning to grind to a standstill (exactly what Al Qaeda had hoped to achieve). The impact of terror on the US was frightening to behold and it spawned an attitude of cold-blooded intolerance that persists to this day. As the dust settled, the President emerged from his bolt hole, and the grieving for the dead of the Twin Towers turned to fury. The sleeping giant had awoken and found that, as far as intelligence and knowledge of the enemy was concerned, it was woefully inadequate.

The US intelligence community, as it exists today, has its roots in Pearl Harbor. The US knew about the Japanese attack but all the elements of intelligence were in different places and "owned" by different military and civilian groups. There was no single agency in place with the right to analyse the material and make the obvious conclusion. So the Central Intelligence Agency was born and divided into two main Directorates: the Directorate of Operations, which gathers information, and the Directorate of Intelligence, which analyses it. Sounds sensible, doesn't it? Well, sadly, it's not. After 1946, dozens of other intelligence gatherers began to evolve. The National Security Agency (NSA), which has a much larger budget than the CIA, is responsible for intercepting signals, such as mobile phone calls and radio signals. Then there is the National Reconnaissance Office. Its job is the gathering of image intelligence from strategic reconnaissance aircraft and NSA satellites, which it supplies to The National Geospatial Intelligence Agency (NGA). The Military and the CIA also have their own image collecting agencies. The Pentagon is responsible for the Defence Intelligence Agency (DIA), which has its own human intelligence service called Defence Human Services and which, at the same time, receives intelligence from the CIA, NSA and NGA. Its job is to concentrate on enemy military capabilities – not easy when you are dealing with an amorphous and indistinct organization like Al Qaeda. In addition, the armed forces all operate their own intelligence-gathering agencies, which concentrate on tactical matters but which coincidentally gather all sorts of other material.

There are also a series of civilian law enforcement organizations operating in intelligence gathering. The FBI deals with counter-intelligence as well as law enforcement and also has a counter-terrorism responsibility. There is a contradiction at the heart of the FBI's anti-terror role. The Bureau is staffed by policemen whose job it is to solve crimes that have already happened. In fact, the Bureau is assessed on its record for solving crimes. Counter-terrorism is all about stopping a criminal act from happening in the future. You collect intelligence, analyse it and predict the outcome. Other agencies such as the Alcohol, Tobacco and Firearms (ATF) Department, The Drug Enforcement Administration (DEA) and Customs and Border Security (CBS), all collect intelligence and use it to facilitate arrests and prosecutions. The State Department is responsible for the Diplomatic Security Service (DSS), a counter-intelligent agency responsible for the protection of US Embassies. The Defence Department runs the Office of Special Plans (OSP). This elite bunch of spooks is small, powerful and has ample resources. It consists of a group of respected intelligence analysts and has the ear of the Secretary of Defense. The OSP and its frequently oblique opinions, was listened to more closely than any other group during the aftermath of 9/11.

It is fair to say that the amount of knowledge retained in the United States by military, state and civilian organizations was out of control in 2001 and the intelligence analysis situation was a disaster waiting to happen. There was no single unit in the United States where all the information gathered by its agencies was collected, analysed and assessed. After the calamity of the Twin Towers it became immediately apparent that the admirable thinking behind the creation of the CIA after Pearl Harbor had been abandoned long ago. Vested interests had taken over and once again "the intelligence community" was just an uncoordinated mess of competing agencies desperately mining data and keeping it to themselves. The knowledge was there, as was the motivation, dedication and technology. So how were nineteen Arab terrorists able to live, train and operate in the land of the free without anyone noticing, before hijacking four aircraft to such devastating effect?

As the new Director of US National Intelligence, John Negroponte has a $40 billion budget. His job is to manage and bring together the fifteen state-funded intelligence agencies operating in the US and forge close alliances with foreign agencies, particularly in the UK. His responsibilities have been wrenched from the grasp of former Defence Secretary Donald Rumsfeld. Negroponte, a career diplomat with little experience in the intelligence world, is now one of the most powerful men in America and his job is to use his diplomatic skills to force and cajole American spooks to co-operate, to encourage them to stop competing and work together for the national good. It is not an easy task and unless he manages to pull it off, American military and civil intelligence, which have taken a severe battering from the media, politicians and the public since 9/11, particularly over the war in Iraq, will probably never recover. Three other senior figures were approached before he accepted the appointment, but all turned the job down.

Negroponte was born in London in 1939, the son of an English mother and a Greek shipping tycoon. He grew up in Europe but was educated in New York, where his family settled after the war. He finished his education at Harvard Law School and joined the Foreign Service in 1960. His second posting was as a political officer in Vietnam, which he says was a "career defining experience". One of the experiences he no doubt remembers is the Phoenix Programme run by Bill Colby from the CIA station in Saigon. It was a dirty-tricks campaign using CIA Assassination squads to imprison, intimidate and kill members of the communist-led government established by the Viet Cong in the rural south. Phoenix resulted in the deaths of many thousands of innocent Vietnamese, and posters charging Colby with murder were plastered throughout Washington DC by the anti-war movement. In the 1980s, Negroponte was appointed US Ambassador to Honduras during the Reagan administration and was accused of ignoring human rights abuses committed by the CIA as they helped the Contra rebels to overthrow the left-leaning Sandinista regime in neighbouring Nicaragua. There were allegations that he knew all about and tolerated the death squads and also Battalion 316, a murderous unit run by the rebel Nicaraguan general Gustavo Alvarez Martinez, and that the Americans co-operated in assassinations and torture. Negroponte denied the charges that had been brought against him in the American media. But they still continue to surface from time to time. During his years in Central America, he adopted five orphaned Honduran children, saying, "I have taken them under my wing, because they'll keep me young. We decided to adopt all the children from the same country because life's complicated enough without having siblings from all over the world."

His diplomatic career has taken him throughout the Middle East, Europe and south-east Asia and he has become fluent in Spanish, Greek, French and Vietnamese. The last step in Negroponte's fiery diplomatic career was as US Ambassador in Baghdad, where he was sent to replace American Proconsul Paul Bremer. However, his hard edge seems to have been softened in Iraq and his record in the country has been a model of sensitive diplomacy. He is no longer seen as a "hawk", but as a reliable civil servant with a "can do" reputation. His patron in Washington is Colin Powell.

Negroponte has taken control of, among other agencies, the CIA and the FBI, and he will need all his diplomatic skills to form alliances between the two. One of the most sensitive programmes he will be expected to oversee will be CAPPS11, a passenger screening programme initiated immediately after the attack on the Twin Towers and so sensitive and secret that it had to be discreetly and temporarily dropped during the 2004 Presidential elections. The objective of CAPPS11, as described by the newly formed Department of Homeland Security, was to create an "automated system capable of integrating and simultaneously analyzing numerous databases from government, industry and the private sector which establishes a threat risk assessment on every air carrier, passenger, airport and flight". In other words it was an attempt to predict and detain potential terrorists, using all the intelligence material the Department and its agencies could get their hands on.

Many travellers who have been to the US for a short break in recent years will be aware of the unpleasant procedure of passing through immigration. It tends to be slow and deliberately intimidating; a reminder that in the land of the free, the rednecks have inherited the Earth. Like most other agencies, the Department of Customs and Border Protection justify their boorish behaviour by describing it as "part of the vital duty of saving American lives". Arriving at Kennedy Airport recently, I was fascinated by a tall, shaven-headed, steely-eyed, armed and uniformed agent who appeared in the hall before the assembled masses of visitors and holidaymakers and loudly berated a young man who had the temerity to use his mobile while he was queuing to be assessed. We had been waiting for over an hour and were forced to listen to the official as he screamed his abuse. It was a clear indication of the level of contempt he had for us poor travellers. A girl travelling with me was hauled off to a back room and interrogated. "It happens every time I come here," she said when she finally emerged, showing me a letter from the US embassy in London which apologized for a fault in their records of her travel to and from the US. "My employers, an airline, has written dozens of times asking for the data to be corrected, and we've sent lawyers' letters, but the immigration officials just ignore them."

In Britain, an increase in terrorism and violent crime coincided with a dramatic reduction in police efficiency and a corresponding widespread move toward private security. When it comes to crime prevention, our police are now largely useless. They are handicapped by bureaucracy, health and safety regulations, the risk of litigation, compensation culture, a terror of being accused of institutional racism, a huge volume of new offences generate by the EU and New Labour legislation, and the dead hand of political correctness. Morale is at an all-time low as successful prosecutions plummet and Human Rights legislation and Data Protection loads the odds against the law. The Data Protection Act of 1998 is divided into 75 sections and contains provision for ferocious penalties against companies and individuals who are convicted of failing to follow its provisions. Failure to observe the Act can result in a fine of £5,000 for each offence. It has never been properly tested in the courts and the means by which it is to be enforced are not clear. The secret filming of an individual without his or her knowledge is unlawful and the material and knowledge gained is not acceptable for use as evidence in court. The policeuse private security firms to protect themselves and their premises against organized crime, as do the armed services, Customs and Excise, most ministries, including Defence, the Banks and all the financial institutions. The British police are considered by their Continental equivalents to have degenerated into one of the least effective forces in Europe, if not the world, while the technology developed and marketed through the British security industry is world class.

The police and security agencies use close surveillance sparingly because of its high cost and extensive use of man-power. A highly trained branch whose services are available to both police and secret service units and who are identified only as SO23 is available to provide close surveillance with the approval of a senior officer and, in some cases, by a civil servant or a minister. The secretive police organization CIB, based in Vauxhall, is tasked with the job of policing the police themselves. It has the benefit of almost unlimited funds with which to stamp out any hint of corruption within the force. CIB is staffed by often reluctant police officers, known to be above suspicion, but concerned at the possibility that their colleagues may become aware of where they are working.

The National Hunt jockey Jamie Osborne, after his arrest on suspicion of corruptly fixing races, was approached by an ex-Thames Valley CID officer named Robert Harrington, who told him that he could ensure that the investigation would be dropped and no charges brought. Osborne went straight to the police and was recruited by the CIB as an *agent provocateur* in a bid to trap Harrington. On the day before Harrington's visit to Osborne's cottage, SO23 cordoned off the buildings and the wooded garden and started work installing listening devices and cameras both in the cottage itself and in the grounds. Trained officers were camouflaged and hidden in the garden to act as protection in the face of any possible threat to Osborne and as possible future witnesses. I have listened to the tapes and seen the film, all of which were used in Harrington's eventual trial at the Old Bailey, where he was convicted and jailed. Cameras with fibre-optic lenses and microphones were hidden in the chimney breast and in the kitchen of the cottage and listening devices were hidden throughout the garden. The site was cleared and cordoned off when the surveillance experts arrived and when, afterwards, they returned to remove the equipment. Harrington was also recorded in a variety of other locations, at great expense in terms of manpower and electronic resources, but the transcripts and film of his meetings with the jockey played a crucial part in his conviction.

There has been significant growth in small, privately run international intelligence agencies, and a corresponding growing demand for discreet boutique companies such as Hakluyt, established by ex-MI6 operative Christopher James, whose knowledge of emerging nations and the third world is legendary and who has expert knowledge about where power lies in any country and how to establish your company in difficult parts of the planet. Hakluyt cultivates a rakish glamour about its operatives, and employs a board groaning with retired field marshalls and a staff of young field agents operating in the most dangerous corners of the globe, where even the most intrepid businessman might feel insecure. Stratfor, a global intelligence agency founded by George Friedman, is known in the US as the "Shadow CIA", because it mixes media reporting and analysis with intelligence consultancy. It is basically a vast information-gathering network and has become a powerful influence in the worldwide intelligence community since 9/11, with its excoriating analysis of American intelligence shortcomings.

Private security has flourished largely in response to the insurance industry's demands that their customers protect themselves from burglary, theft and violence. The insurance industry is able to insist that its risks are covered by an appropriate level of measures. The fact is that sophisticated surveillance techniques and the necessary finance is available to the fast-growing, hi-tech security industry. The profits are huge and the industry is uncluttered by the procedural and budgetary problems faced by the police. The security industry has thus become competitive and innovative and flourishes as it operates profitably not just in protecting the private sector but in the business of guarding state institutions as well. The consequence of this has been to galvanize the security companies. Organizations like Kroll, Control Risks and Hakluyt have expanded to operate successfully in the worldwide intelligence community.

Kroll International is a detective agency run from New York by Jules Kroll, specializing in electronic surveillance and intelligence. The company operates in twenty countries and employs nearly 2,000 specialist staff. International branches of Kroll work for governments including Thailand and South Africa. For example, tt helped to establish The Scorpions, an internal security force inaugurated by Nelson Mandela, the former president of South Africa. The company is retained by businesses that require the intelligence advice and muscle power necessary when operating in difficult international markets. Kroll is probably the biggest and most sophisticated agency of its type and has a reputation for being skilled at tracking down the secret treasure chests of corrupt politicians and international criminal organizations. Its services are expensive. The British company, Control Risks, based in Victoria Street in the City and established by the travel company Hogg Robinson in 1975, is a consultant on corporate security. General Sir Michael Rose is a director and the agency specializes in evading kidnap and assassination, and the screening of job applicants. Control Risks employs four hundred staff around the world and works closely with the security agencies in the UK to protect British commercial interests.

In addition to the manpower-intensive security services that operate mainly "on the ground", since 9/11 governments throughout the world have started to allocate huge budgets to monitoring and intercepting electronic communications. In the US, the interception and interpretation of signals by the Department of Justice, the FBI and the Drug Enforcement Administration intrudes into all forms of communication systems now including broadband internet access and Voice Over IP. As members of the public chat on the phone, surf the internet, or engage in routine on-line transactions, they unknowingly leave behind a trail of personal details that is automatically captured and retained in computer logs. The technology that makes this possible is truly awesome – and can appear in some unexpected places.

Menwith Hill in North Yorkshire comes under the auspices of the NSA and makes no pretence toward spin or public relations. Its function is unashamedly unfriendly and it is accountable to the President of the United States and his national security advisers alone. It is the interface between the American military and the branch of intelligence waged in space and it has a facility to listen in on every signal and conversation carried out in Europe, North Africa and Western Asia. The more you learn about the Menwith Hill Station, the more nervous you become. It's a significant piece of the American war machinery tucked away in The Dales, and one of the most secret places on Earth. Without the very highest level of clearance, no one is even allowed through the gates. The Americans don't even admit that it exists and refuse to allow any visitors, including MPs and MEPs, to enter, even on formal occasions. The Labour MP Alice Mahon said in Parliament that no one concerned about civil liberties can ignore Menwith Hill. Despite many attempts to get answers to her questions, it is quite clear that the base is not accountable to MPs and therefore not accountable to the British people. Although it is an American surveillance installation it was renamed RAF Menwith Hill in 1996 in an attempt to disguise what this powerful military resource is all about. It is not unique, however, and there are similar, although smaller, stations in Australia and Austria.

The base is impossible to hide, you can't bury it or put it underground. You see it on the horizon as you leave Harrogate on the A59 and drive into the Yorkshire Dales. From a distance, it's a collection of large, white hemispherical "radomes" sitting in what was once peaceful moorland. The domes contain satellite receiving dishes and are surrounded by "hardened" (bombproof) buildings. Menwith Hill is the largest electronic monitoring station in the world and has twelve hundred US civilians and servicemen working there. The NSA, which controls the base, has also hired a limited number of carefully vetted British civilian staff from GCHQ. The base has grown over the years and its power and importance is underlined by the closure of other UK-based stations run by NSA. Its official new designation as Regional Sigint (signals intelligence) Operations Centre responsible for running remote, automated intelligence gathering sites emphasizes the strategic importance of the base.

The reason this overt reminder of the dangerous world we live in makes me nervous is that it intercepts all the communications "traffic" passing into, out of and through

Britain and originating from or destined for Western Asia, North Africa and Europe. This base is vital to the Americans because the satellites positioned to provide communications from these regions are "visible" from Menwith Hill but not from the US. "Traffic" comprises all the phone calls, mobile and satellite messages, emails, faxes, radio signals and every other type of electronic communication known to man. If a signal passes along a cable or through microwave radio links or satellites, this station has the means to collect it, analyse it, process it and automatically relay it back to the United States.

The Menwith Hill Station played a major role in the invasion of Iraq in 2002, intercepting and channelling command information. The war was essentially fought by the Americans as a space war in which the allies were able to call on fifty satellites to support the British and American military effort. Twenty-seven global positioning satellites were used to log the location of special operations units and targets, and the remainder were used to channel communications and commands and to warn of missile attack, meteorological weather patterns and much more. General Judd Blaisdell, Director of Space operations for the USAF, stated that around 33,600 people, working at 36 SIGINT stations worldwide, were involved in "space war" activities. Satellite surveillance was supported by data supplied by AWACS – large communications aircraft loitering on the edge of space – and human intelligence.

The systems were by no means foolproof. A number of Tomahawk cruise missiles were wildly off target during the Iraq invasion, and the availability of radio bandwidth was found to be inadequate. The last war in Iraq was a refinement of the techniques used during the Gulf War in 1991. All smart bombs and weapons were controlled by global positioning satellites in space and it is apparent now that space systems are the key to future US military power. At the end of the military action in Iraq in April 2003, speaking at the inauguration of The 614th Space Intelligence Squadron, at Vandenberg Airbase in California, Commander Lieutenant Colonel Earl White remarked that the use of space technology had been a major enabler in the war. "Without space, we're back to World War II," he said. "Whoever takes us on is going to have to take us on in space."

The Base at Menwith Hill was a big military asset during both wars against Iraq. It retains a major responsibility for intercepting and channelling military intelligence and command information, in addition to its functions in data mining, harvesting and analyzing civil and commercial intelligence. Its role can only expand as America develops more space-based fighting systems. The base covers an area of about twenty acres and controls fifty-six satellites from a series of radomes known as "The Runway", which operates in a line from east to west across the southern end of the site. Currently, the base runs two systems – "Silkworth" and "Moonpenny". The Silkworth system, operating from a long, low building in the centre of the base, houses a computer network monitoring satellites stationed over the equator where they intercept long-distance radio communications from Eurasian targets and relay them back to the base. The technology also allows staff to listen to messages and conversations passing between individuals and companies throughout the Middle East and Europe. These are relayed from the satellites Mercury, Magnum and the more advanced Orion. These satellites, like almost all modern communications satellites, are "geosynchronous" – that is, they remain in fixed positions relative to the Earth. The data is downloaded and passed for analysis back in Yorkshire, where it is sorted according to special criteria in a radiation-hardened underground facility called "Steeplebush 11".

The special operations "Moonpenny" or "Sprinkler" systems intercept and receive unauthorized satellite communications from other countries. They consist of a series of interception terminals designed to harvest signals from national and international communications satellites under the control of other states including "Arabsat" and "Intelsat". The scale of the collection process is impressive. NSA aims to collect all international and most national communications. In 1992 the system was intercepting two million messages per hour, of which all but around thirteen thousand were discarded before being refined down to the two thousand that satisfied forwarding criteria. These were whittled down to twenty communications that were selected and examined by analysts. Fifteen years ago, Menwith Hill station was intercepting seventeen and a half billion messages a year, of which around seventeen and a half million could have been analysed.

Echelon is a global intercept system, also administered by the NSA, which captures and analyses virtually every phone call, fax, email and telex message sent anywhere in the world. It is operated in conjunction with GCHQ at Cheltenham, the Communications Security Establishment (CSE) of Canada, the Australian Defence Security Directorate (DSD), and the General Communications Security Bureau (GCSB) of New Zealand. These organizations are bound together under a 1948 agreement, UKUSA, whose terms and text still remain secret. According to an investigating European Union Committee in 2001, the Echelon system provides British and American analysts with data gathered by 120 spy satellites. This means that every minute of every day the system can process three million electronic communications. Echelon is simple in design; it intercepts stations all over the world. It captures all satellite, microwave, mobile phone and fibre-optic communications traffic, and processes the information through the computer capabilities of the NSA, which include advanced voice recognition and optical character recognition programs. NSA staff also search for code words or phrases (known as the Echelon "Dictionary"), which prompt the computers to flag the message for recording and transcribing for future analysis. Intelligence analysts at each of the respective "listening stations" keep separate keyword lists to help them analyse conversations or documents flagged by the system, which are then forwarded to the intelligence agency that asked for the intercept. Echelon is also reputedly being used to intercept domestic surveillance against American civilians for reasons of "unpopular" political affiliation or for no obvious cause. If this is true, it amounts to political spying and is in violation of the First, Fourth and Fifth Amendments of the American Constitution.

The European Parliament's report entitled, "An Appraisal of Technologies of Political Control", issued by the Scientific and Technological Options Assessment Committee of the European Parliament, asks whether Echelon communications interceptions violate the sovereignty and privacy of citizens in other countries. There is little doubt that Menwith Hill conducts surveillance against British citizens on their own soil and with the full knowledge and co-operation of the British Government.

Echelon was created with the assistance of GCHQ at Cheltenham and, in 1993, disaffected elements in the UK intelligence community used the network to leak details of US attempts to win votes at the UN in favour of intervention in Iraq. The British intelligence community was deeply unhappy about Government attempts to distort intelligence information by claiming, falsely, that Iraq had maintained links with the terrorist network Al Qaeda. A twenty-eight-year-old woman employed by GCHQ was arrested on suspicion of breaking the

Official Secrets Act. She was said to have leaked a memo from the NSA asking for information from "product lines" (Sigint jargon for wiretaps and email interceptions) ordering an intelligence "surge" directed against Angola, Cameroon, Chile, Bulgaria and Guinea with "extra focus on Pakistan UN matters". Written by Frank Coza, Defence Chief of Staff (Regional targets), the memo had simultaneously been circulated by the NSA. The operation, probably authorized by National Security Adviser Condaleeza Rice, would also have involved Donald Rumsfeld and CIA Director George Trenet. President Bush would certainly have known about it. The leak was a carefully planned act of defiance that illustrated the unhappiness throughout the security services regarding the way British and Americans were misusing intelligence. The rift with senior intelligence operators had been festering for some time and had not been improved by revelations that UN Secretary General Kofi Annan's office had been bugged by the Americans.

The facility at Menwith Hill continues to grow, however, and has completed much of the work on the Space-Based Infra Red System (SBIRS) for which even the NSA was forced to apply to Harrogate District Council for planning permission before it could be installed. There are no missiles or other air defence systems in place, although there is little doubt that, in the unlikely event of a nuclear strike, the base would be a prime target. SBIRS is "Star Wars" by another name. Four new satellites have been launched into orbit to replace four redundant orbiting vehicles from the Defence Support Programme. Among other advances, the new system is able to track "cold bodies" in space as well as infra-red signatures caused by burning rocket motors. In a speech to Congress, the American general Howell M. Estes III, Commander in Chief of the North American Aerospace Defence Command, said that SBIRS systems will improve the American ability to "provide much more precise launch and impact point of theatre missiles to forces in a theatre of operations". In other words, the accuracy and ferocity of American firepower controlled from space gets more effective every day.

The fear and anger induced by the secrecy surrounding Menwith Hill has naturally created political resentment. Speculation about what the Americans are doing on British soil is never-ending. MEPs regularly demand to know exactly what is going on at the base and whether the Americans have been given access to European trade secrets, which they obviously have, and whether this is jeopardizing European job security. It is certainly hard to imagine the Americans tolerating a similar British or European facility on their soil and difficult to understand why this NSA base should not be accountable to the British Government.

Local resentment to the Menwith Hill station is more than just a Yorkshire shrug and a muttered "nowt to do wi' me, lad". Local people want to know what is going on behind the razor wire and why such a huge base fails to generate any local employment. The few technicians and analysts from Cheltenham who are stationed there are the sum total of British involvement. The scene outside the base is reminiscent of the anti-war protests at Greenham Common. There's the constant presence of weather-beaten ladies from the local Yorkshire CND camped outside making tea on fires lit from chopped up bits of garden shed. They've been there for years already and are cheerfully aware that they're in for a long wait. Protesters regularly trespass inside the base and their activities serve to highlight the US military's general lack of humour or understanding when it comes to demonstrations of this sort. The result is that, from time to time, something happens that shows that even a war facility can have its ludicrous side.

When two women, Helen John and Anne Lee, were appealing against a conviction for trespass at York Crown Court in 1997, a BT solicitor was called as witness. The representative managed to let slip that the company had installed three optical-fibre cables with the capacity to carry more than 100,000 telephone calls simultaneously to the American base. The BT solicitor, presumably incorrectly briefed by his client, provided the appeal court with details of the cables and was then instructed to withdraw his evidence by the judge. The old "Post Office" – BT's predecessor – had originally provided two-high capacity "wide bandwidth" circuits to Menwith Hill in 1975. These were connected via coaxial cable to the BT network at Hunters Stones, a microwave radio station close to the US base. During the 1970s and 1980s almost all Britain's long-distance phone calls were routed through Hunters Stones. BT was now admitting that the cables were connected directly to the United States through an undersea cable. The company said in evidence that the capacity has since been trebled by the addition of two more optical-fibre links.

The BT solicitor also claimed that other telecommunications companies in Britain have supplied tapping capacity to the American base and that British companies were involved in spying activities at Menwith Hill. The revelations by the BT solicitor came to an abrupt end with the judge's intervention, who accused the witness of giving away national secrets. BT sent a second lawyer along to try to have the evidence prohibited. The appeal thus turned into farce, but a corner of the British surveillance curtain had been lifted, albeit briefly, to reveal that our own government is supplying the Americans not only with military intelligence but with commercial secrets as well, and that British companies are doing the work.

Data sourced from British businesses is daily being made available for analysis at Menwith Hill.

GCHQ, the Government's listening station at Cheltenham, is described as a "crime fighter" by the Joint Intelligence Committee that is responsible for it. In fact, the true role of the base is as one of the world's most sophisticated intelligence gatherers. In 2004, it moved to a new site on the outskirts of Cheltenham that had been purpose-built as a secure listening station at a cost of £1 billion. The security of the information transmitted from GCHQ is the responsibility of the Communications Electronics Security Group (CESG). Sigint is intercepted by the Composite Signals Organization, which has offices at Cheltenham as well as in Cornwall and on Ascension Island.

GCHQ provides intelligence to all the security services and shares it will Menwith Hill and the NSA. In fact the organization shares staff with the Americans and uses the same methods to "flag up" satellite and other types of electronic intelligence into and out of the British Isles. GCHQ participates in the American Echelon system using the Echelon dictionary to capture "product" – useful intelligence information. Much of GCHQ activity is restricted to British intelligence agencies but the organization was heavily involved in preparing for the war in Iraq, which caused dismay among many of the 3,500 staff working at Cheltenham – hence the disaffection and leaks.

This form of intelligence gathering is intended to be entirely covert – the assumption must be that the subject of electronic "eavesdropping" is unaware that he or she is being spied upon, otherwise the information gathered is worthless. But there is a more direct – and cold-blooded – way to extract information from terrorist suspects: torture. Of course, torture conducted on US and UK soil is strictly against the law. But if you are an intelligence-gathering organization that has the full support of the highest people in the land, there is usually a way round minor problems such as illegality. The CIA and the NSA, desperate for an analysis of the terrorist threat, produced lists drawn from the interrogation of Afghanis and other known Middle Eastern suspects. The administration was demanding results and wanted them quickly. The CIA started to increase the use of what it calls "Rendition". This is a peculiarly cynical American creation that has been supported shamelessly by the British. What concerns us here is "Extraordinary Rendition", a euphemism for leaning on someone else to do your dirty work for you.

The practice, when described in cold dispassionate terms, sounds like a tale that has been written down by Franz Kafka in the saloon bar just before closing time. What makes it peculiarly alarming is that it is carried on with the full knowledge and enthusiastic co-operation of the British Government. American officials admit that Extraordinary Rendition has been used by the CIA at least two hundred times, which almost certainly means that it has been used considerably more often, but that is the only figure they are prepared to admit to. It is known that individuals have been kidnapped around the world, their clothes cut off with knives, their bodies stuffed with sedative suppositories, their wrists and legs chained, their faces masked and hooded, their bodies wrapped in diapers and clothed in orange jump suits. Like cargoes of meat, they have been transported in Gulfstream executive jet aircraft to states including Egypt, Morocco and Uzbekistan where the extraction of information by means of arm-boiling, water-boarding, battering with hammers or the attachment of electrodes to the genitals are everyday occurrences. In other words, Extraordinary Rendition is simply a euphemism for forcing suspects to confess to involvement in terrorism by subjecting them to torture. The only imaginable reason that Americans are prepared to do this is that they believe the end justifies the means. They are convinced that the people concerned are committed terrorists and that, as law enforcement organizations are bound by strict rules of procedure in their own country, they do not have the legal means to subject their suspects to the level of physical and emotional pressure necessary to force them to talk quickly.

The quality of intelligence raised by physical and mental torture is known to be inferior. A Special Branch officer I talked to, who has had lengthy experience of interrogating IRA suspects, commented that "you can persuade someone to say anything in the hope that you will stop causing him or her pain. It doesn't mean to say that it's the truth". He continued, "There are quicker and far more efficient ways of getting at that. Torture as a means of obtaining meaningful intelligence just does not work." The reason behind the American recourse to such savage and unjustified action is twofold. Firstly, the legal process in the US is long winded and thorough, with lengthy appeal processes and constant referral to human rights. The penal system in the US is known to be brutal, but only to those who have been convicted of crime. Guantánamo Bay in Cuba houses suspects who have no legal representation and can be treated as if they have no civil right at all. As far as the Bush administration is concerned, terrorists are not protected by the Geneva Convention, but, to avoid embarrassment, suspects are kept away from the homeland and any possibility of legal interference and are imprisoned in secret installations controlled by the CIA throughout the world. The American enforcement agencies involved are judged by results and a confession, even under duress, is considered a bonus. Also the fear of capture and secret delivery to an underground cell in a secret barracks in Cairo will concentrate the mind of even the most fervent "freedom fighter" and word of the horrors awaiting anyone suspected by the CIA has spread fast throughout the Arab world.

Earlier this year, George W. Bush was asked about the practice of Extraordinary Rendition carried out by agents of the CIA during a White House press briefing. He backed away from the question, looked downwards, paused, glanced sideways around the room, coughed and then muttered that the practice existed but was justified because "it was an anti-terrorist measure and there was nothing he would not do to prevent the loss of American lives". Two months earlier, on January 27, in an interview with the *New York Times*, Bush had said, "Torture is never acceptable. Nor do we ever hand over people to countries that do torture." This was a bare-faced lie.

There is, unfortunately, too much evidence of the practice of Extraordinary Rendition to have any doubt that it is taking place. What is worse is that by using such extreme methods, the USA is dragging its friends and allies down with it. The aircraft used and operated by the CIA, under the cover name of Premier Executive Transport, are regularly refuelled in Royal Air Force bases and Civil airports throughout the UK, and the material extracted by the torturers is passed on, considered and analysed in cold blood by British intelligence operatives. The main problem faced by the teams of aircrew and thugs referred to as The Special Removal Unit who carry out these transfers during their programme of flights around the world has been, of all things, the great British plane-spotter. This slightly potty pastime has developed into a large and very efficient network of members. A Gulfstream with the registration number N379P was traced by plane spotters to an aircraft charter business called Premier Executive, a paper company with its headquarters in a lawyers' office in suburban Massachusetts and a chairman with a listed address in Arlington, Virginia close to CIA Headquarters. The aircraft was logged regularly in and out of the UK and is known to have landed at Brize Norton, Mildenhall, RAF Leuchars, Luton and Glasgow. Its movements in and out of the UK have been noted down with great diligence by spotters and recorded on their databases, according to Chris Yeats, an expert in aircraft movements. Its presence here was either to refuel or take part in the process of "Rendition" from the UK to less benign environments in Africa and the Middle East. American intelligence agencies habitually use civil aircraft flown by civilian companies for their operations as a means of avoiding the attention military jets generally receive. The CIA, however, failed to factor the British plane spotter into its calculations.

Once journalists discovered that a private aviation company was acting as support for the CIA and started to ask questions, the head office address and the registration details of Premier Executive Travel were immediately changed. Private aircraft with CIA agents on board are also known to have landed at Broma Airfield in Sweden, where special forces seized two Egyptians from a suburban street in Stockholm. The men were thought to be associates of Al Qaeda and were held in Sweden for eight hours before being drugged and flown straight to Cairo, where they were imprisoned and subjected to months of torture and interrogation. One of the men, Dr Aziza, managed to get to a telephone and call his wife Hanna before he was drugged by the Special Removal Unit. Dr Susan Fayed, a medical worker at Nadim, a solitary Egyptian refuge and rehabilitation centre for victims of torture, told me that they deal with people who have been in prison and released suffering from fractures, burns and paralysis after torture with electricity. She says that Dr Aziza was seen by his mother after the torturers had started work on him and he was in a shocking state. He has since been sentenced to twenty-five years hard labour. His associate was released and lives under house arrest in Cairo. He remains too frightened to talk about his experiences. "The Americans know what is going on here," says Dr Fayed. "Many of the victims seen at the Nadim Centre have been delivered here by the Special Removal Unit."

Craig Murray, the British Ambassador to Uzbekistan, a nasty little dictatorship sandwiched between Afghanistan and Russia, became aware that he was under surveillance when he was invited to dinner with Professor Jamal Mirsaidov, a human rights activist in Tashkent. The next day, Mirsaidov's grandson was found tortured to death. He had been beaten with iron bars and boiled. The Uzbekistan authorities claimed he was the victim of a drug overdose. Murray became concerned when he discovered from a conversation with an MI6 agent that the British security services believed that the intelligence being passed to the CIA and MI6 from Uzbekistan was of the highest quality and considered reliable. He returned to London in 2003 to protest to his superiors in the Foreign Office, who took legal advice from one of their own law officers, a Mr M.C. Wood. Mr Wood confirmed that it was legal to "possess information gained by torture". Murray talked to Foreign Secretary Jack Straw, who told him that he, "was losing sleep over it," but had to follow the advice of the intelligence services.

Quite apart from the moral implications of the current, "no-holds-barred" form of intelligence-gathering, it is my belief that the American and British security services are vulnerable to farce and cock-up like everything else. This is particularly true of surveillance. Spooks like to say that only the failures and cock-ups are noticed because everything else is secret. That may well be true, but how are we to know? The Americans, for instance, famously failed completely to predict the Al Qaeda attack on the World Trade Center – despite the fact that Osama Bin Laden had already attempted to destroy the building once before, by having one of his men plant a truck bomb in the basement. In fact, US and UK intelligence failures go back much further than that. American intelligence not only missed Pearl Harbor, but also the fall of the Berlin Wall, and had no idea about Kruschev's decision to send missiles to Cuba until the weapons were photographed *en route* by a U2 spy plane. British spies failed to predict the closure of the Suez Canal by Egypt's president Gamal Abdel Nasser, which sparked the Suez crisis in 1956. They were unprepared for the start of the mainland bombing campaign by the IRA, the fall of the Shah of Iran, or the Argentine invasion of the Falklands. When it comes to finding out details such as where Mugabe keeps his looted millions or in which roof space a drug dealer is growing his skunk, we certainly have the knowledge and ability to get to the truth. We also know a great deal about the habits and foibles of our own subjects, because – as we have already seen – we are the most watched country in the world, by far. But when it comes to the detailed prediction and analysis of the big events, we don't seem to have the skill to sift, scrutinize and plan, and neither do the Americans.

This inability to predict the major event, in spite of the information owned by the agencies operating on behalf of the state, is mainly due to the failure to analyse what has been learned through intelligence, and this is principally due to the quality of personnel employed in the security services and the "human factor" – simply making mistakes. Throughout the major powers the obsession is more with collecting information than analyzing it. It is this lack of unity and clarity of purpose, and lack of insight among the various agencies involved that results in the often calamitous political misjudgments that come to light after the event. The CIA's published mission statement is to provide accurate, evidence-based, comprehensive and timely foreign intelligence related to national security, and conduct counter-intelligence activities, special activities and other functions related to foreign intelligence and national security as directed by the President. If the objective is for the intelligence to be evidence based, who sets the parameters? And what level of evidence is required to justify the "special activities?" Of course, this mission statement may well have been written by a little man in beige chinos sitting in Madison Avenue and the term "special activities" may have caught his eye and given him a thrill. You never know.

We do know, however, that the US Intelligence Community has a budget of $40 billion a year, but still seems to miss the big stories. And so do we. The issue of intelligence failures will be looked at in more detail in Chapter Nine.

Chapter Seven: Eye in the Sky

We all have a vague idea that there are sophisticated pieces of metal called satellites in orbit above our heads and that they are, generally speaking, a good thing. As well as being used to explore space, they bring us television from around the world, and provide global positioning satellite (GPS) navigation systems and powerful telephone resources. They watch the weather and can even follow the progress of sand storms in North Africa. Satellites are also used to trace the movement of fish and animals as they move around the earth – the Chinese use satellite surveillance to monitor the migration habits of their population of four thousand black-necked cranes, for example. The European Union checks that the "set aside" land for which farmers are paid benefits is left fallow and the progress of forest fires is monitored across the globe, from the Greek Archipelago to the Amazon.

Satellite surveillance has been highly effective in helping to curb oil pollution caused by the once widespread practice by commercial shipping of cleaning their tanks at sea. In 2005, there were thirty-one satellites in orbit capable of imaging the land surface at resolutions of from one to thirty metres. Of these, fourteen are privately funded by US corporations, all with resolutions of ten metres or better. The cheap commercial satellite systems now becoming operational provide images with even higher resolution, and they will become an important aspect of consumer marketing as they monitor the movement of goods around the globe. But isn't it disturbing to think of the "see-all eye in the sky" that can pick out any one of us from a crowd and watch us for as long as it chooses – wherever we go? How can we protect our privacy from such a remote but highly efficient system that operates in a medium not subject to the rule of law or of democratic vote? Countries all over the world – and most especially the United States – spend huge sums of money on miniaturizing the technology of snooping. As a result, the spy camera does not have to be in orbit in space to see what you are up to – it could be hovering in a corner of your room.

Of all spying systems, it is the thought of being watched by satellites that makes me most nervous. It is bad enough that there are cameras in the streets and in the shops, and intrusive forms to fill in for government agencies such as the Inland Revenue, and that I have to prove my identity every time I turn up at Kennedy Airport for a holiday, but the knowledge that something invisible in space is able to identify me and my friends and record everything we do, is truly nerve wracking. Of even greater concern, if they can put equipment into space to monitor our every move without us having any say in the matter, what else can they put into orbit above our heads, and what will that be able to do? The scientific advances brought about by the "space race" and Ronald Reagan's "Star Wars" initiative have been staggering, and the US is now talking about fighting wars in space.

America's most powerful means of spying on its enemies and its citizens is the KH ("Keyhole-class") satellite. These cost $1 billion each, and yet all that is known about their movements in space is that they operate at different altitudes from other satellites – details of their orbits above the Earth are highly classified. The exact number of "Keyholes" in operation is unknown, too, although it is generally accepted that there are around two hundred of them in "fixed" orbit (that is, moving at the same speed as the Earth and so remaining in the same position relative to the ground beneath) and that there are tight clusters of them positioned over trouble spots such as the Middle East and North Korea.

Artificial satellites are designed to perform specific functions. A communications satellite, for example, usually carries an umbrella-shaped dish structure with multiple antennae. The "Keyhole" fleet is the key to the success of Echelon, the greatest intelligence gathering system of all time, and also to the development and use of weapons in space. "Keyhole" satellites are launched into orbit aboard NASA space shuttles or Titan 4 rockets. They are, essentially, orbiting digital cameras equipped with very high powered lenses capable of resolving objects on the ground as small as 12cm across. This means they can read a car numberplate, or the headline on a newspaper, or identify a clip of ammunition. The camera software scans the object and either records it immediately, or, if visibility is poor, makes an automatic decision to produce an enhanced image. The images the satellites transmit are analysed at the National Imagery and Mapping Agency, which distributes the data to government security agencies on demand.

Data gathered by "Keyhole" satellites are theoretically for use in military intelligence gathering and scientific research. The NSA and CIA are beneficiaries of the data, however, because it is known from evidence given in US courts that law enforcement agencies have used the hardware to spy on US citizens considered "potential terrorists, lawbreakers or troublemakers". In other words, just about anyone can be targeted as a subject for observation by the satellite fleet in orbit above the Earth.

The science involved in sending sensors and sophisticated filming equipment into a stable orbit above the planet has developed at a fast rate since the early days of space travel, and "lifting" systems to place satellites in space now operate from launch sites all over the world. Some of the machinery in space has the capability to carry out sophisticated, and occasionally aggressive, tasks. That so much effort and so many resources should be put into the science of satellite technology is perhaps understandable considering the impact that the first artificial satellite, the Soviet Sputnik, had on US morale when it was launched in 1957. At the time, the Sputnik caused a huge level of concern bordering on panic in the United States. Even though Sputnik did little more than broadcast "beep beep" noises from a cheap radio is it flew over their heads, Americans felt that their airspace was being violated – and it left them feeling extremely vulnerable. The technology today is much more sophisticated that that. From five miles up, the modern spy satellite can watch and record all our day-to-day activities. It has heat sensors and image-enhancement technology allowing it to carry on watching us, wherever we are. It makes no difference whether a target is walking down the street, or driving at speed along an autobahn, or is even indoors – down in the basement, or deep in the interior of a fortress. The weather makes no difference, either. The subject could be sitting in a prison in the middle of a thunderstorm.

Although there are numerous spy satellites in orbit, it actually only requires three of the most up-to-date versions to "see" the entire world. As well as having the power to capture and transmit pictures back to earth in real time, what else can they do? Can they control earthbound electronic surveillance systems from orbit, or overhear our conversations from space, or deploy weapons even? The Americans relied heavily on satellite technology during the Afghanistan and Iraq Wars. It allowed them to intercept vast quantities of communications data through their Echelon system and deliver it back to the CIA's headquarters in Langley, Virginia, via GCHQ, Menwith Hill and many other stations.

The Americans are not the only nation with surveillance satellites orbiting the earth, of course. Space is now cluttered with hardware busily recording and transmitting, or just circling the earth as airborne hulks. There are currently three thousand artificial satellites operating in orbit above the Earth. The Astra satellite fleet, which transmits programmes for B SKY B, has twelve satellites orbiting at 22,300 miles from the Earth. Of the two hundred American "Keyhole-class" satellites launched since the early nineties, nearly one hundred and fifty are believed to still be operational. The remaining fifty are redundant and have joined the six thousand items of space junk orbiting the world.

Thanks to the wide availability of high-resolution satellite imagery from unrestricted civilian sources, even the less prosperous nations can obtain instant access to satellite surveillance, provided they pay for it. Images of obvious military value can now be acquired by virtually any country. In fact, although few nations can afford to conduct their own spy satellite programs, IKONOS, Quickbird and other private systems are affordable by virtually all countries – and their quality is of a high enough standard that even the CIA and the NSA make use of them.

It is spy and military hardware that provides most of the "Sigint" and photographic data devoured by the intelligence agencies and police forces in Britain and America. When you see the images they are able to transmit back, it is almost impossible to believe the distance from which they were taken. The American government department most heavily involved in satellite surveillance technology is the Advanced Research Projects Agency (ARPA), an arm of the Pentagon. NASA is concerned with civilian satellites, but there is no "hard and fast" line drawn between civilian and military functions. The National Aeronautics and Space Administration (NASA) launches all US satellites from either Cape Kennedy in Florida or Vandenberg Air Force Base in California, whether they are military-operated, CIA-operated, corporate-operated or launched by NASA for experimental reasons or space research. It is difficult to make a quick distinction between government and private satellites; research by NASA is often applicable to all types of orbiting hardware. Neither the ARPA nor NASA are in the business of manufacturing satellites; instead, they underwrite the technology while various corporations produce the hardware.

The American military currently limit their satellite activity to surveillance, navigation and communications. But it seems certain that they will expand their capabilities to having weaponry in space at some point in the future. One of the stated reasons for this is that commerce is already active in space – in the form of communication satellites – and so will need safeguarding. Wherever US commerce goes, so does US national interest and the need to protect it. In 2002, Paul Teets, the Undersecretary of the Air Force and Director of the National Reconnaissance Office, said in a speech that he believed weapons will go into space and "it was just a question of time". Teets probably knows what he is talking about because of his experience in the development of precision-guided weapons such as missiles and bombs that can be accurate to within a metre. Laser-guided bombs and GPS-guided missiles, such as the Tomahawk, have already given military forces an immense capability that can ensure the defeat of any known enemy in a conventional war and, with correctly deployed satellite technology, can cut out collateral – that is civillian – damage, at least theoretically. The trend is toward more precise and lethal weapons systems, often unmanned, that are able to respond within seconds to attack targets anywhere on earth that have been identified by "Keyhole" satellites. On this basis, space technology and the use of satellite guidance will provide significant advantages in future warfare. The US Government, after its successful experience with space technology in waging a war in Iraq, is now actively pursuing research on the next generation of weaponry – laser and "kinetic" weapons. (We'll look at what they can do shortly.)

According to the *Washington Post*, the US President and his military commanders have accepted that some sort of conflict in space is now inevitable and are preparing for it. The Clinton administration's restrained approach to "Star Wars" systems has been replaced by the Bush administration's unquestioning acceptance of the inevitable exploitation of space for military purposes. It is an alarming prospect. The technicians are not only working out ways in which we can be watched from space, but are also planning ways of using space technology to kill us.

Cost, however, remains the major problem. Satellite lift in the United States is expensive. This is why commercial satellite providers use the launch facilities in countries such as China, where it is cheaper. One of the most important non-US sites is Baikenour in Kazakhstan. In order to operate satellites tactically, so that they can move from low orbits to high, you need enormous amounts of energy. High-power generation systems are also needed to fire and maintain weapons that use high-energy lasers, thereby avoiding frequent and costly re-fuelling. There has been much interest in forms of technology that can help to decrease the size of future space platforms and so reduce the amount of lift they will require. Tiny devices, called micro-electromechanical systems (MEMS) will be able to sense heat, light, motion and sound and can be used in a number of space applications including surveillance and the control of reflective mirror surfaces in space-based laser systems.

Each weapon system that is developed and deployed will require a complete "system of systems" in order to integrate surveillance, acquisition, tracking and battle damage assessment. The United States foresee constellations of satellites, which would be less vulnerable to attack, whereas if just one satellite was used an attack on it might disable the entire system. Several constellations, in low earth orbit, could provide global, "24/7" coverage. This means the world's population could be under constant threat from orbiting weapons linked to surveillance systems.

Laser weapons are about to become part of the superpower arsenal. Chemical oxygen-iodine lasers have already been designed and built that also have weapons applications. Chemical lasers have been under development since Reagan proposed the "Star Wars" missile defence system back in the eighties. During the last twenty years, these weapons have undergone significant improvements in optics, miniaturization, power generation, beam control, and targeting by means of surveillance satellites. The technology exists to produce a prototype that would allow targets to be engaged within seconds or minutes – anywhere in the world. The American Air Force is about to deploy this type of laser in its Airborne Laser system (ABL). Designed for ballistic missile defence, it is soon to be put into operation on a regular basis. The disadvantages of the ABL is that it needs to be airborne during an expected attack by ballistic missile to be effective. This is what makes a space-based laser weapons system – on permanent standby – the military's preferred option. A space-based laser would provide constant coverage, if enough of them were deployed. Lasers are not all-weather weapons systems, however. Clouds, rain, and atmospheric effects can scatter the laser's beam, necessitating increased power output to compensate. But lasers are flexible weapons in that the amount of damage they cause can be controlled by the duration of the pulse and the power of irradiation. Flammable materials will catch fire under fairly low irradiation levels, making targets such as petrol refineries particularly vulnerable. At higher-power levels and longer duration (which would amount to several seconds) the laser may be able to burn through and destroy a more solid target. High-powered lasers have already proven effective in shooting down ballistic missiles during their "boost" phase – when they are packed with fuel in order to overcome Earth's gravity. Once adequate advances can be achieved in high-power generation, and miniaturization techniques are employed in order to solve the weight burden of lifting the device into orbit, space laser weapons should be readily available for production and deployment.

There is a second space-based weapon system being developed by the Americans, using what is called "Kinetic" technology. Kinetic weapons are projectiles launched from space-based platforms and guided by GPS or laser designator. Kinetic weapons are extremely accurate because they use similar guidance systems to those employed in precision-guided bombs and missiles – but without the explosives. The missiles achieve their great destructive potential by virtue of the speeds they can reach. By attaining hypersonic velocities they can produce enormous forces that are capable of shattering virtually any target. It is claimed that a Kinetic weapon is able to destroy targets such as command or ammunition bunkers buried hundreds of metres underground. Single or multiple targets can be attacked depending on the type of projectile employed.

Unlike lasers, Kinetic weapons will be all-weather devices, capable of being launched from satellites and striking targets anywhere on earth in a matter of minutes. This gives them a huge advantage over lasers. Another advantage is that Kinetic weapons do not require the vast amounts of power that lasers need. They would work in conjunction with "Keyhole" surveillance and targeting satellites and will be launched from one of a cluster of satellite weapons, making them very difficult to attack. The main problem with kinetic weapons is the heat that they generate upon re-entry, which can seriously damage the electronic GPS receiver needed for guidance. One possible solution being tested currently involves the use of lasers to create a "bow wave" to shield the projectile as it passes through the atmosphere. It is impossible to defend yourself against a kinetic weapon after it has been launched. The only defensive measures that might be feasible against Kinetic attack would be to use anti-satellite weapons. These could disrupt the GPS navigation systems needed to guide the weapon or eliminate the satellite before it can launch the projectile. The technology to produce Kinetic weaponry is already available. Any future improvements in technology will simply increase its accuracy and destructive power.

As a significant factor in influencing a conflict's outcome and totally eliminating the need for conventional weapons, they will not necessarily alter the balance of power. It is likely that, ultimately, space weapons will become just another conventional precision-attack weapon system, providing support to other weapons, rather than replacing them.

War waged from space will allow commanders, who will of course be remote from the battlefield, to use unmanned satellite systems to run the surveillance, identify the target and destroy it. Space weapons will have a truly global reach. The first part of this programme likely to enter space is the network of surveillance satellites required to identify the targets. These will be more powerful than anything that has existed before, able to see into every corner of the planet.

There is good reason for international unease at the potential devastation caused by a war waged from space. All tactical targets would be vulnerable to attack. Due to the quick reaction and speed of laser weapons, tanks, aircraft, armoured vehicles, missiles, helicopters, and ships, nearly any surface-based military target can be engaged and destroyed. Ships at sea will no longer be immune from attack in any part of the ocean. This type of global reach has not been seen before. Although, B-2 stealth bombers can apply force with precision anywhere in the world, the time it takes to reach its target is far slower than the speed of delivery from space.

While it is possible that space weapons may play a role in military action at sea, peacetime presence and crisis response missions, including amphibious contingency operations, will never disappear. The Navy will have a viable and significant role to play. Aircraft carriers, as the showpiece of national diplomacy and the centre of rapid response operations, will continue. Of course, they will become increasingly more difficult to defend and, as technology improves, the time will come when there will be nowhere to hide. Eventually, all nations will need to play a part in controlling space in order to safeguard their use of the sea, air and land. Therefore any US monopoly on the deployment of offensive weapons in space would be temporary at best.

Obviously, the deployment of offensive satellite systems in peacetime will create a huge international row. All nations that do not regard themselves as allies of the US will consider it necessary to try to develop defensive systems. Intrusive surveillance from the fleet of "Keyhole" satellites will be the first target. In China, some potential defensive countermeasures are already on the drawing board. These measures are, no doubt, rather limited at the moment because of the high costs of development and installation involved but are likely to improve over time. In recent months, attempts have been made to jam American surveillance satellites. Space warfare control, including anti-satellite warfare, will clearly have an impact on future military strategy and planning. The US has historically resisted placing any anti-satellite weapons systems in operation, so it is expected that a system would remain ground-based. Whether space-based or ground-based, the US space warfare control mission will have to be expanded. The commercial use of space is extensive, especially in the domain of communications. Opening space up to potential conflict would devastate American industrial and commercial activities. Simply put, denying the West access to commercial communications satellites would bring the American economy to its knees very quickly. In general, however, all such futuristic visions do not turn out quite as expected. Space weapons may be a formidable asset to the commanders of the future, but a general will still continue to rely on conventional resources. Just as nuclear weapons have not removed the requirement for a robust conventional capability to include navies and armies, it is obvious that space-based offensive weapons will not satisfy all the needs of the military, and anyway, as we have discussed, counter measures are already being developed against them.

Information technology and the huge amount of data which is now heavily relied upon by field commanders now comes predominantly through satellite communications. Even so, it is frequently insufficient. The US is investing heavily in back-up systems, using Unmanned Aerial Vehicles (UAVs) which are capable of providing real-time surveillance, intelligence, and targeting information. Their job is to become alternatives to satellites or the old-fashioned proved "Predator" drones which proved invaluable for forward surveillance in the Iraq war. British companies are supplying video and GPS systems for use by the American scientists developing surveillance robots. University College in London has developed a reconnaissance vehicle in the shape of a snake that is designed to move across the ground in the manner of the reptile it mimics. It will be dropped from a pilotless aircraft and carry instruments capable of transmitting details of enemy positions. Its computer can adapt so that it will continue to operate even after it is damaged. Unmanned aerial vehicles (UAVs) have been developed to scout buildings, tunnels and caves. Powered by contra-rotating fans and equipped with sensitive visual, acoustic and infrared devices, they float about the urban battlefield and transmit intelligence back behind American lines.

A variety of UAVs of all sorts, such as "the Predator", are now a familiar sight over Iraq. They are cheap, discreet and tend to be used mostly for surveillance and intelligence gathering. But the trend is towards much smaller devices. Microscopic flying devices have been in development since 1995. The goal during the past five years has been to mimic a flying insect, both in flight and size. For example, the way that a butterfly moves in flight is well understood and can be copied by scientists. Prototypes have been built and flown successfully. Twenty years ago, American companies such as Aeronvironment were designing and testing tiny flying machines powered by lithium batteries and with a payload of a video flight computer, camera and transmitter. The early models like the propeller driven Black Widow was 15cm long and weighed 56g. It was capable of producing a pin-sharp image. Modern miniature flying machines naturally remain secret because they are in use, not just by the security agencies but for covert reasons, by private companies. Clearly one spin-off from military research into the private sector will be the ability to use micro robotics as a means of carrying such sophisticated surveillance systems into heavily protected environments.

Two or three years ago the US Office of Naval Research built and tested a prototype spy drone that was smaller than a penny. Recent variants are even smaller and more powerful and use solar power to drive four membrane wings that flap at a rate of 180 beats per second, which enables them to create lift. The wings carry what is called "smart dust" – microscopic computer chips that are the brains of the vehicle. There have been reports in the US of minute, remotely controlled, mass-produced flying insects manufactured and developed by the Georgia Tech Research Institute being used to infiltrate buildings and remain unseen. The technique is called "biomimetrics", which means the mimicking of biological systems and adapting them for human requirements. The "insects" are capable of transmitting data over long distances. Some are used in guidance systems and adapted for fast and inexpensive mine-clearance projects. They are designed to take advantage of poor weather to reach long distances into enemy territory. Other concepts have been developed using miniature jet motors fuelled by hydrocarbons and able to fly over ten kilometres at eighty km/hr. RMB Miniature Bearings, a Swiss company, manufactures electric motors that weigh one third of a gram. And scientists at the Massachusetts Institute of Technology have developed a jet engine measuring 10mm by 3mm that is powered by petrol or kerosene.

Of course, these are toys for spies and the real dirty work is being perpetrated by the listeners with their code-breakers and their massive computers bolted down in dust-free rooms in remote rural landscapes round the world. The science of miniature robotics and the use of smart dust has been in development for several years and the Pentagon has remained silent about how far the research has progressed. There is no doubt that the techniques they have been working on have produced dividends in both intelligence gathering and battle-field surveillance. The problem is, these machine will have to be operated by men told what to do by politicians. That is where it will probably go wrong.

Military and commercial technologies develop along separate lines but regularly join up for mutually beneficial applications. Advances in civilian remote surveillance technology applied to the modern battlefield have meant that warfare has already reached a stage of development bordering on science fiction. The impetus for what has become known as "remote warfare" lies with the Americans who have a clear-sighted attitude to armed conflict uncluttered by the moral scruples that dog other nations. Unlike the British who have taken to prosecuting their soldiers for killing Iraqis during military actions against insurgents, the American priority has remained the safety of their forces and their citizens. Even when a soldier was caught on camera cold-bloodedly shooting three unarmed wounded prisoners it did not result in any charges being brought. The US has never signed up to the International Criminal Court, and if an American soldier says that he felt that he was under threat when he opened fire, it most unlikely that he would ever be prosecuted. In fact, there have been no criminal prosecutions of American servicemen taking part in combat during or after the Iraq War. This attitude enables them to develop weapons technology that might not be acceptable to the UK armed forces. The introduction of robots as both surveillance devices and killing machines is one example.

The use of pilotless aircraft as missile launch vehicles has now become a common occurrence. The robotic warfare development programme – Special Weapons Observation Reconnaissance Direct Action System (SWORDS) – and the weapons it has developed have seen action in combat situations in Afghanistan and Iraq. Early in 2005, the Americans started to send armed robots into Iraq. The robots were primarily designed to carry out a reconnaissance role in enemy territory but they also had the capacity to shoot to kill. These early robots are actually remote-controlled tracked vehicles that can be operated from a distance of one thousand metres by a soldier using a laptop computer. They carry GPS navigation systems, cameras, and rapid-fire automatic weapons – and some variants can be armed with grenade launchers and anti-tank missiles.

A machine will kill without remorse or guilt and will be fast. The Pentagon has allocated $70 billion to military robotics in a programme called "Future Combat Systems" and with this sort of investment and the rapid speed of technological development, it is inevitable that robots will soon be used as a matter of course. The British, however, are concerned about the ethics and legality of robotics on the battlefield. In August of 2004, an RAF pilot, using a computer-based system at a USAF base in the Nevada desert, was able to control a Predator drone flying over Iraq two thousand miles away and launch a Hellfire missile into the target – an insurgent group stronghold.

An ex Head of Strike Command told me, "We train our pilots to assess and identify targets before opening fire. The RAF pilot operating the Predator in the US was acting under British law and rules of engagement. But we are concerned about the effectiveness of remote-controlled weapons in a crowded urban battlefield. Could we guarantee that a robot would able to distinguish between an armed insurgent and a woman with a baby in her arms? How can you programme a robot to make lightning-fast life-and-death decisions in chaotic battle conditions? A soldier has to rely on instinct and training and must make difficult and instant judgments. I don't think you can expect a machine to do that effectively yet. We would be worried about the possibility of an armed machine malfunctioning. The science of combat robotics is still in its early stages and relies on technologies such as radio signals and image transmission which could easily be interfered with."

Revolutionary changes in the way war and surveillance are conducted in the next century cannot solely be predicted based on the presence of offensive space weapons, robotics and the development of miniature surveillance systems. Ultimately, war always comes down to human conflict – man against man, the essence of battle. The ultimate goal of robotic research is to produce a machine that can do everything a soldier can do. The Americans estimate that the eventual cost of a robotic soldier will be about 10 per cent that of its human counterpart. At the moment, the technology, according to Geoff Grossman, a researcher with the US Joint Forces Research Center, can provide computer processing "brainpower" equivalent to that of a mammal.

Anti-satellite weapons will have a significant place in future military planning using space-based or ground-based technology. No country has actually admitted to planning anti-satellite weapons systems, certainly in space. But the development of laser and kinetic weapons is going ahead and may soon mean the use of weapons in space, which would lead to yet another arms race. There are no easy answers. At the moment, the US and the UK with Echelon technology siphoned through its Keyhole satellite fleet have achieved the greatest breakthrough in intelligence-gathering the world has ever seen. Now they are discussing how to arm the surveillance system.

There are many questions to be answered by the US policy-makers and military planners. For example, will the US be able to afford new space war systems – and are they worth the investment? Will other nations refrain from matching US efforts in space once the United States breaks the moratorium on weapons in space? And will offensive space weapons threaten the stability of the world? Many would argue that it is time to agree a ban on all weapons in space. Satellite technology and warfare means that a new set of rules for the conduct of war would have to be devised and new strategies developed by those responsible for the conduct of war.

Installing offensive space weaponry in orbit will be controversial, not just in the US, but everywhere. Politicians and academics will debate the issue before the "Final Frontier" becomes a battleground. It is likely that the American public would support defensive space weaponry, such as anti-satellite systems, especially following 9/11. Indeed, many Americans seem to believe the desire for privacy, bearing in mind what they see as the current threat from "global terror", is already futile and that the use of more intrusive satellite surveillance technology and the deployment of space weaponry is a foregone conclusion. The US could then become the first nation to break the voluntary international moratorium on placing offensive weapons outside the Earth's atmosphere. The unilateral arming of space would be a disaster for relations between the US and her allies around the world. Although no actual treaties would be broken, any remaining belief that the US would be willing to abide by the same rules of international conduct that other countries follow would be gone forever. The great fear of many countries is that if space militarization was to creep in because of an apathetic American electorate, the potential consequences are devastating – it could destroy the planet. It is fair to say, however, that the Bush administration hasn't seemed too concerned. It seems inconceivable that space weapons should ever gain the destructive power of nuclear weapons. Deployment of nuclear weapons in space would potentially mark the beginning of the end for the human race. But because "space war" is still only in its early stages, nuclear weapons might still be regarded solely as a deterrent. Politicians will no doubt use the excuse that nuclear weapons in space would only be used in remarkable circumstances. But who would decide what those circumstances would be?

Chapter Eight: Law and Disorder

British police forces are faced with a new piece of criminal legislation every three days. Of course it's difficult to keep up with such a drain on your resources because it comes wrapped up with bureaucracy, codes of conduct, test cases and all the paraphernalia that accompanies new legislation. There has been an enormous amount of law created since 9/11, both in the United Kingdom and the United States. The UK has the Prevention of Terrorism Act, the US has the Patriot Act. Both pieces of legislation have appeared alongside other overt signs of heightened security measures including increased surveillance of the population. Faced with fanatics who, we are told, will kill ruthlessly and indiscriminately, both governments have said they must bring in much tougher legislation to ensure that the killers are removed from the streets and kept away from society.

This legislation is highly controversial, however. As there is often insufficient evidence to secure a conviction against terrorist suspects, the new laws allow the state to lock people up without trial. Therefore it is seen as illiberal and against long-held British and Americans tradition. Inherent in these laws is the widespread mining and storage of personal information and intelligence on the citizenry. In the UK, the Data Protection Act and the Freedom of Information Act are there to protect us, and, theoretically at least, to enforce our right to know precisely what data others have stored about us. How secure does all this make us feel?

The Bush administration, constantly chanting the mantra of "making the saving of American lives a priority", has tried to turn the US into a fortress and has thrown away the civil rights rule book in the process. The brutality against Arab prisoners at Abu Ghraib and elsewhere was deliberate policy. Defense Secretary Donald Rumsfeld made it clear that US forces would do whatever was necessary to extract information from anyone they believed might have knowledge of plans to attack the United States. The sexual humiliation of Arabs is an effective method of coercion. Arab society often holds the victim of sexual torture responsible for their fate. And so the revelation of that abuse, to the community from which the victim comes, is worse than the abuse itself. The men and women responsible for the abuse were either obeying orders or displaying the violent and dark side of the American soul.

As I wandered round the streets of Manhattan recently, I stopped for coffee at Starbucks and picked up a copy of the *New York Times*. I read that the CIA has now actually admitted to torturing prisoners in Iraq and elsewhere round the world and that The Justice Department was reviewing a number of cases where prisoners have died in custody as a result of interrogation by the Agency. PJ Goss, the Director of the Central Intelligence Agency, told Congress in March 2005 that all interrogations "at this time" were legal. He declined, when pressed, to make the same broad assertion about practices carried out during the time that has elapsed since September 11, 2001. A legal opinion issued by the Justice Department in 2002 followed a narrow definition of torture. This allowed the agency to resort to a broad range of coercive techniques against suspected terrorists being held in undisclosed locations throughout the world without being guilty of "torture". Not to put too fine a point on it, the CIA has used interrogation methods that are considerably more brutal than any used by the military or civilian law enforcement agencies. The Agency's use of "Rendition", in which suspects are handed over to countries like Egypt and Syria that are known to be prepared to use any form of physical or mental coercion has been covered. The CIA seems to feel that sending suspects off to the third world to be brutalized is a way of keeping its hands clean.

The United States "Patriot Act" became law during the chaotic aftermath of September 11, having been rushed through Congress without debate, just three weeks after the tragedy. It was signed off by President Bush on October 26, 2001 without a House, Senate or Conference report. It is, by any standards, a draconian piece of legislation in which the phrase "Patriot Act" is the public relations title for what is actually named "The Uniting and Strengthening America by Providing Tools Required to Intercept and Obstruct Terrorism Act of 2001". The legislation is a compromise version of the Anti-Terrorism Act of 2001, and introduced dozens of constitutional changes to increase the operational powers of the intelligence and law enforcement agencies. It contains provisions that will extend the rights of the state to monitor and intercept private communications and even gives the FBI access to sales by booksellers and library records, from which they can form their own opinion of a citizen's political beliefs.

The "Patriot Act" permits the US Government to intercept information transmitted over the internet and to interfere with an individual's civil liberties with the use of evolving technologies. It also permits the law enforcement agencies to use new communications technology without reference to Congress, and this has grave implications for the citizens of many countries outside the United States, particularly Canada and Great Britain. The Act has many provisions relating to electronic surveillance that were proposed before the destruction of the Twin Towers and which were, at the time, the subject of a great deal of criticism and debate. One of the consequences of 9/11 was the immediate silencing of any meaningful opposition to the civil liberty implications of anti-terrorism measures. The Bush Administration brought pressure to bear by making it clear that it believed that further attacks were imminent and that without the "Patriot Act" the Government would be hamstrung and unable to respond. The Attorney General, John Ashcroft, allowed members of Congress just a week to debate and pass the Bill, stating that if they did not, then Congress would be responsible for subsequent terrorist atrocities. John Podesta, Clinton's White House Chief of Staff between 1998 and 2001, has remarked that overnight the Congressional mood had changed from extreme caution to willingness to allow the law enforcement agencies to "return to an era where they could monitor and harass individuals who were simply exercising their First amendment rights".

Only one senator, Russ Feingold, opposed the Act during the aftermath of 9/11. He said that he was certain that the increased law enforcement powers to engage in electronic surveillance would be improperly wielded. "To the extent that the expansive new immigration powers which the Bill grants to the Attorney General are subject to abuse, who do we believe is most likely to bear the brunt? Not immigrants from Ireland, El Salvador or Nicaragua; or even Haiti or Africa. It will be those from Arab, Muslim and south Asian countries who suffer. Our Government has been given vast new powers and they may fall most heavily on a minority of our population who already acutely feel the pain of this disaster."

It would be incorrect to give the impression that the monitoring of electronic communication around the world was regarded by the US as solely their responsibility. The US Government has put pressure on all democracies to enhance their wiretapping laws to involve new and future technologies. Terrorism is a global problem, and so any initiative against it must have a global dimension. Soon after 9/11, former FBI Director Louis Freeh was employed by the Bush administration to travel to emerging countries in Eastern Europe, Asia and Africa to sell the idea of wiretapping. The US has also promoted the desirability of making sure that all wiretapping technologies are manufactured with built-in surveillance capability. In other words, they wanted to prevent and make illegal the manufacture of any communication or surveillance equipment that cannot itself be spied upon and listened to.

Most democratic countries, however, understand that eavesdropping on its citizens is not generally regarded as popular or desirable State behaviour and have built safeguards into their legislations and constitutions. The UK, the US and most other democracies are legally bound to publish the numbers of wiretaps that have been authorized each year. They have firm regulations in place to ensure that intercepts are authorized by a judge, and even then only after a series of strict conditions have been adhered to. Intelligence and law enforcement agencies are, in theory, forbidden from initiating eavesdropping activities before demonstrating that other methods of investigation have been attempted but were not successful. France and the UK have established independent commissions to monitor the abuse of wiretaps. The members of these commissions are highly qualified in the use of communications and intercept technology and have the power to investigate all those involved in surveillance and – most important of all – to ask awkward questions. Other countries, such as Canada, have appointed Privacy Commissioners with statutory powers to examine the use or misuse of state surveillance.

Some countries publish annual reports on the use of state surveillance broken down by government department. These include Australia, France, Canada, New Zealand, Switzerland, Sweden, the US, and the UK. But some are showing reluctance to publish the figures. Holland, for instance, has recently relaxed its regulations on the reporting of wiretaps. It may seem, on the surface, surprising that such a traditionally liberal country should do this. But the assassinations of the liberal politician Pim Fortuyn and the radical film maker Theo Van Gogh have hardened attitudes to Islamic extremism in Holland. It is perhaps no coincidence that the Dutch have both the highest percentage of legal and illegal immigrants and the highest number of wiretaps in the European Union. As yet more countries enter the European Community allowing more non-nationals the right of entry into member states, and Turkey – the first truly Muslim country – teeters on the brink of joining the EU, there is a growing backlash by primarily Christian countries of the EC to set up barriers against what is feared may be the start of a cultural and religious take-over.

The responsibility of the monitoring bodies overseeing wiretaps extends not just to inquiries about the interception of intelligence from the states in which their powers lie, but also to the surveillance of communications traffic and inter-ference with electronic information throughout the world. The listening posts at GCHQ Cheltenham and the US facility at Menwith Hill in Yorkshire eavesdrop on a global scale, and most democracies have an equivalent secret monitoring facility.

The published lists of surveillance operations provide instances of electronic surveillance use and detail how long they were in place for. The main justifications for such surveillance come under two main headings – crime and terrorism. The lists of wiretaps are published to demonstrate that acceptable activities such as journalism, environmental activism, human rights, trade unionism, religious activities and political opposition are exempted from unwarranted surveillance and that these groups are not being targeted just because they may have a conflict of interest with whoever is in power. It must also be clear that the detection of petty crime is not subject to intrusive surveillance for political reasons. Making the security services accountable to the electorate by monitoring them in this way is vital in a true democracy.

You don't have to be a conspiracy theorist to have doubts about the state abuse of wiretapping and the routine interception of correspondence. Article 17 of The Commission on Human Rights requires that "the integrity and confidentiality of correspondence should be guaranteed, *de jure* and *de facto*. Correspondence should be delivered to the addressee without interception and without being opened or otherwise read. Surveillance, whether electronic or otherwise, interception of telephonic, telegraphic and other form of communication, wiretapping and recording of conversations should be prohibited".

The British Security Services registered a total of 540 wiretaps in the United Kingdom in 2004. Yet the debate on the Anti-Terrorism Bill made it clear that eavesdropping in the United Kingdom for the purposes of law enforcement was constant and widespread. In fact the case for locking up terrorist suspects without trial and without informing them of what they were suspected of and why, was, according to the then Home Secretary, David Blunkett, justifiable on security grounds. In other words, if a suspect knew what evidence there was behind his incarceration, he would be privy to how the security services gained this information. "Intercepts are not permitted to be used as evidence in court and I am not in favour of permitting their use," he said. In truth, most eavesdropping carried out by the security services is outside the law and the people who do it do not want to have to justify their behaviour under cross-examination in court.

There is no such reticence in the United States. The "Patriot Act" is deeply unpopular in many parts of the US because of the ways in which it sidesteps the safeguards put in place to prevent the misuse of state surveillance. In February 2004, The New York City Council passed a resolution condemning the infringements of privacy rights inherent in the legislation. Authors and librarians have campaigned against Section Five of the Act, which permits surveillance of library records. The scope of the powers available to the FBI has gradually become apparent in the years since it was enacted. The recorded number of secret surveillance warrants in 2004 increased to over two thousand, many more than the number of Federal wiretap warrants that had been taken out, simply because the "Patriot Act" has made secret surveillance of innocent people far easier to justify. There has also been deep concern north of the US border, in Canada. In November 2004, the Privacy Commissioner of British Columbia released a report alleging that personal information on Canadian citizens had become subject to seizure by the US under the Act and that it violated Canadian privacy laws. Complaints about the interception and analysis of private British communications traffic aided and abetted by BT and controlled by the NSA at Menwith Hill fall on deaf ears.

The detailed implications of the increased power of the state have gradually become clearer as the public begins to realize what is going on. There are three laws within the Act that are relevant to the interception of communications by the US Government. Title 111, relating to wiretapping or real-time interception of voice and data communications, requires "probable cause", and the approval of a judge. It is an important safeguard requiring a high legal standard. The Electronic Communications Privacy Act (ECPA) concerns the installation of "pen registers" (which collect outgoing numbers from a specific phone line) and "trap and trace devices", (which collect incoming numbers on a specific phone line). These can be used to record all web and email activity from a private individual's telephone line. This Act does not require "probable cause", but use of the devices requires a court order, which can be acquired by a government attorney certifying to the court that the information is relevant to an ongoing criminal investigation. Thus the Act makes it easy for the Government to access private financial information without having to prove that the individual is suspected of being engaged in specific criminal activity. A third law, "The Foreign Intelligence Surveillance Act", permits the use of electronic surveillance against anyone in the US who is believed to be an agent of a foreign power. The surveillance requires "just cause", and a judicial order, but offers less protection to the individual than is required in wiretap cases. The situation often arises where information about British citizens, gained by Americans operating on British soil, is shared with the UK intelligence agencies.

The difference between Title 111 and the Electronic Communications Privacy Act is that the first relates to the content of communications, while ECPA and the use of pen register and trap and trace devices, theoretically relates simply to numbers. Consequently, Judicial approval relies on no more than certification by a government attorney, and the procedures lack the privacy protections required for Title III. The Act that became law in October 2001, however, redefined the "pen register" as "a device or process which records or decodes dialling routing, addressing or signalling information transmitted by a an instrument from which a wire or electronic communication is transmitted" – which includes emails sent through a laptop computer. "Trap and trace" was similarly redefined as "a device or process which captures the incoming electronic or other impulses which identify the originating number or other dialling routing, addressing and signalling information reasonably likely to identify the source or a wire or electronic communication". These "re-definitions" are significant because they mean that huge amounts of private information can now be intercepted and stored without judicial scrutiny, on the mere say-so of a government lawyer. This interception of electronic mail, web surfing and all other forms of electronic communications is known as "Carnivore" and it is at the heart of the "Patriot Act". It is the responsibility of the FBI. The data it collects and analyses is naturally far more revealing than simple phone numbers, but can monitor websites and other information accessed while using the internet.

In July 2000, the US Attorney General, created a Justice Department Review Panel to examine the privacy and civil rights issues surrounding "Carnivore". However, when George W. Bush was subsequently elected President, the panel was replaced by a "high-level official". The review had not been finished by September 11, 2001 and, not surprisingly, Congress did not have the benefit of the review's findings when forced, under pressure, to pass the "Patriot Act".

In addition to the perceived illiberal nature of the Act, there remains an alarming aura of lunacy surrounding it. While it tolerates and encourages law enforcement agencies who intercept communications and eavesdrop on US, Canadian and British citizens, it defers to the gun lobby and appears to put the interests of gun owners before the advice of anti-terrorist agencies, forcing the latter to stand back while terrorist suspects buy arms. In the United States, Islamic fundamental groups, radical militiamen and others known to use violent means to promote their cause have the right to buy arms at will. To deny them this right is considered unconstitutional and a serious infringement of their human rights. The law states that the only groups barred from bearing arms are convicted criminals, illegal immigrants and the insane. The National Rifle Association is one of the most powerful lobbies in the US and is a ruthless defender of the right to bear arms. New Jersey Democratic Senator, Frank Lautenberg blames the Bush Administration's fanatical allegiance to the gun lobby for the anomaly on gun records, and has demanded action. According to the FBI, their agents are restricted from accessing or using gun owner records and have to stand by while terrorist suspects shop for firearms. Former attorney General John Ashcroft has prevented the FBI from matching what it refers to as its "Terrorist Watch List" against data listing all those who have purchased guns. The FBI "Terrorist Watch List" numbers several thousand suspects and no one knows how many have armed themselves since 2001. It is known that at least 47 were granted weapons licences in the nine months after June 2004. According to the FBI, all these applicants were either known or suspected terrorists and were being monitored under the "Patriot Act" legislation. The rules are thus loaded against the FBI who are forced by law to destroy all their records of weapon purchases within twenty-four hours.

The British Prevention of Terrorism Act received Royal assent in Britain on March 11, 2005, after a difficult passage through

Parliament. The Act brought in a system of control orders designed to disrupt terrorist activity. Control Orders allow the Home Secretary to ban terrorist suspects from using the internet or mobile phones, they restrict travel and can ban association with a list of individuals. Suspects may be tagged and subject to house arrest or curfew. It is a tough and illiberal piece of legislation because it applies to all British citizens and removes the presumption of innocence. There are safeguards. The Home Secretary must apply to a Judge in the High Court to make a non-derogating Control Order, although, if it is urgent, he can circumvent the application and refer it to the court for confirmation within seven days. In practice, the Home Secretary can force an individual to remain under House Arrest by opting out of the provisions of the European Court of Human Rights, but it would need to be confirmed by Parliament, following a debate, within 40 days. The Home Secretary's powers are described as temporary and will lapse annually unless they are renewed by a vote from both houses of Parliament. The safeguards also include the appointment of an independent reviewer to report to Parliament on the Act every year, and, at the same time, to report on the use of control orders. The Prevention of Terrorism Bill has been allowed into British law only because it was considered that there is a unprecedented security crisis in Britain. The question is, how long will it be before the Act is repealed and the country returns to normal? Much of terrorist legislation enacted in the past tends to remain on the statute books for years, if not indefinitely.

Anyone who has tried to read the Data Protection Act of 1998 will understand how difficult it is to understand exactly how you can use the law to protect your personal privacy. The 1998 Act is an updating of the 1984 Act and was passed after much debate and deliberation in Parliament. It was, predictably, out of date as soon as it passed into law because of the rapid progress of technology. The Act has a Data Commissioner to enforce it, and it allows recourse to the Human Rights Act. This not only helps the consumer but also often plays a major part in the way the provisions of the Act are interpreted and enforced when a case reaches court. There is a code of practice accompanying the Act and lawyers can make a good living from representing those who believe that their privacy has been violated. At first glance, there seems to be nothing in the Act that states that drivers should be warned if the car they are driving is fitted with a tracker. Neither is there any legislation that imposes a duty of care on the owners of surveillance data. What is the legal position of an organization that gathers images of bank customers using ATMs, which are subsequently stolen by a criminal gang?

Basically, the Data Protection Act covers any personal information that is collected or stored on paper or electronically. For instance, whenever personal data is entered on a website, such as an email address, postal address, age or phone number, the website is legally bound to inform you what it is using it for and must also give you the option of barring them from passing it on to anyone else. They should give a "Use of Data" notice that describes the purpose for which the data is required. When an individual subscribes to a magazine or fills in a coupon on an advertisement, there is generally an option to receive information from "partner" organizations for marketing purposes (usually in fine print). If the subscriber declines, it is illegal to pass on his or her details to a third party. Commercial organizations must only use the information given to them for the purpose stated in the agreement. Websites must state if the information given to them is to be encrypted. And if a database collects personal information, it must store it for the minimum possible time, although this period is not always defined in the Act.

All junk mail in existence relies on someone passing on personal details to a marketing company. The Data Protection Act is designed to protect all personal information, from bank details to NHS records, email addresses and phone numbers. The individual has the right to see details of all the information about him or her that has been recorded anywhere by private or public organizations. Commercial companies must justify why they retain personal data. If they cannot, then it is illegal and must be deleted, by law. The information requested by individuals must be supplied within forty days before it can be reported to the Information Commissioner.

The Data Protection Act also controls precisely what can and cannot be done in the fast-expanding field of surveillance. In Britain, as far as the law is concerned, there are four types of surveillance not covered by the Act. These are, first, targeted and intrusive surveillance activities, which are covered by the Regulation of Investigatory Powers Act and deal with anti-terrorism and investigation into serious crime. Second, the Use of surveillance by employers to make sure their employees are complying with their contracts of employment. Third, security equipment installed by householders for home security purposes, and, last, cameras and similar equipment used by broadcast media for journalism, artistic or literary purposes. The 1998 Act sets out a number of basic standards. The data recorded on CCTV must be fairly and lawfully processed for limited purposes, it must be adequate but relevant, accurate, not stored for longer than is necessary, and should be processed in accordance with an individuals' rights. It must be kept secure and must never be transferred to countries which do not provide adequate protection under the law.

The Data Protection Commissioner can issue Enforcement Notices if he or she considers that there has been a breach of the Act. The code of practice is issued to everyone installing surveillance equipment. It has to be regularly revised to take account of developments in the interpretation of the legislation, technology involved in image recording, and in the use of sound recording, facial recognition techniques and digital technology, all of which are dealt with in the legislation.

When a CCTV system is installed, users must justify their need for it. For example, they may be concerned with the prevention, investigation and detection of crime, arrest and prosecution of offenders, staff and public safety, or monitoring the security of premises. It is an offence to install a system without the legal safeguards listed in the Act. Those responsible for the installation must reveal who they are and give an assessment of the relevance of using CCTV or any other surveillance equipment. They will have to justify their assessment and reasons for the installation. The purpose will be logged with the Office of the Data Protection. They must reveal who is responsible for day-to-day compliance with the Code of Practice and document security and disclosure policies. The way in which images are captured must also comply with the Act and the equipment must be sited so that it can only monitor spaces that are intended to be covered. If there are domestic premises close by, the user must discuss the installation with the owners and receive their agreement if there is any possibility that images from private areas might be recorded.

The operators must only be able to use the equipment for the purposes for which it has been installed. In many CCTV schemes, such as those used in town centres or near large retailers, CCTV systems are often highly sophisticated and tend to direct cameras toward specific activities, or search for particular individuals, or examine recorded CCTV images to search for a criminal or a witness or assess how an employee is behaving. Organizations using CCTV for anything other than the most basic of surveillance must comply with the DPA, but not all their images will be covered in all circumstances. The rule of thumb is that they must decide whether the image they have captured is aimed at learning about a particular person's activities.

If cameras are adjustable, the operators must not alter or manipulate them to overlook spaces that are not covered by the scheme. If it is not possible to restrict the equipment to avoid intruding on people's privacy, the operators must be trained in recognizing the privacy implications of what they are filming. For example, individuals sunbathing in their back gardens obviously have a greater expectation of privacy than individuals mowing the lawn in their front garden. It may be appropriate for the equipment to be used to protect the safety of individuals when using ATMs, but capturing images of PIN numbers and balance enquiries is illegal.

Visible and clearly legible signs have to be placed so that the public are aware that they are in a zone covered by surveillance equipment. There are clear guidelines about the size of the warning signs: they must identify who is responsible for the surveillance, why it is there and who to approach for information. Sometimes surveillance can be carried out without notice, for example, if announcing the presence of the signs would jeopardize a criminal investigation. In which case the system must be dismantled as soon as it is no longer required.

There are strict regulations about the quality of the images obtained as well. If a system has been installed to prevent or detect crime, the images must be adequate, should be regularly tested and conform to quality standards outlined in the Act. A "human monitor" must be in place who is able to assess the match and determine what action should be taken. His or her assessment must then be recorded. If the criminal activity under investigation by this form of surveillance only occurs at night, then constant recording may only be carried out at the appropriate times and using properly maintained cameras. While images are kept, their integrity must be maintained, to ensure evidential value and to protect the rights of people whose images have been recorded. The Act says that images must not be kept for longer than is necessary. For instance, unless they are needed as evidence, town centre images should be erased after thirty-one days. Viewing these images should be in a restricted place and confined to appointed staff only. There are strict provisions for the storing of film that may be used as evidence and for ensuring that the rights of the individual who has been recorded are protected. Any disclosure must follow guidelines laid out in the Act.

If the purpose of the system is the prevention and detection of crime, then disclosures to third parties are limited to law enforcement agencies, prosecution agencies, legal representatives, the media (when the public's assistance is needed to assist in the identification of victim), witness or criminal in a criminal incident, and the people whose images have been recorded and retained.

There are eight Data Protection Principles embedded in the Act that must be followed by anyone involved in surveillance of the public, and the Data Controller is responsible under the Data Protection Act for instituting the surveillance. Of course, the Controller has no influence over covert surveillance or interception of conversations. A glance at spy equipment websites shows the huge range available to the individual who wants to eavesdrop. And it improves every day. Nobody regulates it.

Chapter Nine: Intelligence Failures

Despite the intelligence failings that led to 9/11, the security services of the United Kingdom and the United States are still unable to keep up with national events. A US Commission, set up to look into the security services, reported in April 2005 that not only was the US intelligence community completely wrong in almost every conclusion that it came to before the Iraq War, but it is still in the dark about the current state of the nuclear programmes of hostile states – even though the alleged nuclear ambitions of Saddam was one of the principal reasons given for waging a war against Iraq. Agencies such as the CIA, FBI, NSA and the newly formed Department of Homeland Security still see each other more as rivals than as collaborators with a common mission – to fight global terrorism. For many observers, of even greater concern was the apparent manipulation of the intelligence in the run-up to the Iraq invasion.

Both the CIA and MI5 failed to pass on to policy makers the serious doubts they had regarding one of the key sources of information on Iraq's alleged stockpile of weapons of mass destruction. Perhaps the time has finally come when civil servants provide only what they think their political masters want to see. The case of Algerian terrorist Kamel Bourgass, who was jailed in 2005 for murdering a police officer and for plotting terrorist attacks, is seen as an example of the failure of the UK intelligence and law enforcement agencies, as well as that of other government departments, including the immigration service. Every so often the insurance industry publishes an assessment of the risk of imminent terrorist attack. The threats are allocated ratings such as "elevated", which is bad, and "high", which is worse. The UK, for example, has had an "elevated" risk of attack since the start of the Iraq war. According to the international insurance brokers, Aon, there are currently eight categories of terrorist that may pose a threat to the West, and the UK is up there near the top of the table facing at least four of them. This year Aon says we are at risk of attacks by Islamic extremists, animal rights groups, Irish Republican terrorist groups and organized crime groups. The US is also at risk, but their threat list includes the risk of attack from the far right and religious extremists. The trouble the public faces is just how great is this threat? Politicians are constantly warning that an atrocity is just around the corner, but either it doesn't happen, or it nearly happens but the details are kept quiet so as not to jeopardize the legal process. So what is actually going on? What do recent events tell us?

Despite the UK Government's best efforts, the British public has inevitably become complacent over the terrorist threat. In part, this may be because the British criminal justice system ensures that any information that might prejudice a fair trial is kept out of the public domain until the legal process is complete. Since 9/11 there has been a spate of terrorist "incidents" on the British mainland, yet the public has been kept generally unaware of what is going on behind the scenes. Against a background of general public concern that the Home Office is tinkering with civil liberties, the politicians continue to chant the mantra of "ever-present danger", warning that a state of war exists between the UK and fundamentalist groups and a terrorist threat remains imminent. Because there have been no bomb atrocities in the streets or mass gassings on the London Underground, the public has remained cocooned within, what politicians insist is, a false sense of security and either takes no notice of government and police warnings or dismisses the warnings as lies and hot air. Many of us still remember the outrages of the IRA bombing campaign (and some of us have first-hand experience), but even our memories are becoming blurred over time and so there remains an air of complacency regarding the current terrorist threat.

In the United States, politicians including the President of the United States and Defense Secretary Donald Rumsfeld had spoken about armed Al Qaeda terrorists on the loose in Europe and were somehow associating this with the situation in Iraq to provide justification of their decision to go to war. But the British public have had no facts on which to base a judgment. The reason for the general lack of knowledge about the current terrorist situation in the UK was that there was a series of three interrelated trials in the Old Bailey in progress, which were finally only completed in the spring of 2005. To have released details to the media before the legal process was complete would have been prejudicial to a fair trial, and because of the contempt order placed on the three cases by the Lord Chancellor, all public comment about the issues was forbidden. It was finally acknowledged publicly, in April 2005, that through-out 2004/5, the Central Criminal Court in London had been in a state of permanent high alert as allegations of Islamic terror plots slowly made their way through the system. The evidence steadily piled up that terrorists had been planning to carry out attacks throughout the capital using explosives, a cocktail of poison gasses, and ricin and other toxic chemicals. The privileged few sitting in the Old Bailey and watching the case build up against the terrorist fanatic Kamel Bourgass and his co-conspirators must have wondered what it would take to convince the British public of the peril they were facing.

The charges in the first two trials were brought against eight named men, but there were at least another six who are known to have been involved but who have never been caught, and a number of other activists whose details are unknown. Some of the accused men were trained terrorists, who were associated with the Al Qaeda training camps in Afghanistan, and who worshipped at the Finsbury Park Mosque in North London, using it as a command centre to wage war on the British mainland. The trials have not only revealed the dangers that the British public has faced since 9/11, but have laid out in terrifying detail the ineptitude of the law enforcement agencies sent to investigate and detain the terrorists involved.

Nigel Sweeney QC, counsel for the Crown in the Bourgass trial, presented evidence that proved beyond doubt that the Finsbury Park Mosque was a terrorist centre where recipes for ricin, poison gasses, and explosives were copied and distributed to fundamentalists throughout the UK. The recipes had originally been unearthed in Kabul during the Afghan war and were little more than schoolboy attempts at making poison. Details of terrorist cells, including photographs, were discovered after a tip off by MI5, and used in evidence. In the dock during the first trial, were Kamel Bourgass, Mouloud Sihali, David Aissa Khalef, Sidali Feddag, and Mustapha Taleb. They were charged with conspiracy to murder and conspiracy to commit public nuisance between January 1, 2001 and January 23, 2002. All except Bourgass were found not guilty of terrorist offences. Bourgass was a twenty-seven-year-old science graduate and a product of the Al Qaeda training camps in Afghanistan, whose only previous offence had been a conviction for shoplifting three pairs of jeans in July 2002. The jury took fifteen hours to convict Bourgass of the murder of Police Constable Stephen Oake, the attempted murder of two Special Branch officers and the wounding with intent of Police Sergeant Paul Grindrod. He was sentenced to life imprisonment, with another seventeen years for terrorism-related offences to run concurrently. The trial judge recommended that he spend at least thirty years in prison before he is eligible for parole. As he sentenced him, the judge commented that thirty years was the longest sentence he could pass, as the Criminal Justice Act had not yet become law. Had he the choice, he would have ordered that Bourgass be put away for the rest of his natural life.

The accused in the second trial were Khalid Alwerfeli, Samir Asli, Mouloud Bouhrama, Kamel Merzoug and a fifth man, Mohamed Meguerba, who broke bail and fled to Algeria. All apart from Meguerba were acquitted of terrorism but convicted of immigration offences. The third trial was not proceeded with. Nigel Sweeney told the court, "At least ten named Muslims, together with persons unknown, were intent on bringing death, injury and fear to the streets of Britain in a Jihad holy war." All were illegal immigrants from Algeria who were living in safe houses in Manchester, London, Doncaster and Bournemouth. The planning for a terrorist "spectacular" had started in January 2001 but the breakthrough that saved London from serious outrage did not occur until two years later, in January 2003, when Special Branch anti-terrorist police officers raided a small two-bedroom apartment in Wood Green Lane, North London, and unearthed a chemical weapons factory.

Poisons and gases create public fear and alarm. Inside the apartment, the Special Branch officers discovered ingredients, equipment and instructions needed to make, among other deadly poisons, ricin, botulinum toxin (which causes botulism) and "rotting meat poison", which is as horrible as it sounds. "Rotting meat poison" is considered to be a thousand times more powerful than nerve gas and only a minute amount is needed to cause instant death. Bourgass's supposed expertise with poisons was also underlined by the discovery of recipes for nicotine poison, potato poison and cyanide. A detective described it as kitchen sink bomb-making requiring little more than schoolboy chemistry and using ingredients from the supermarket. In fact it was all a bit amateurish.

All the raw products were easily obtainable. Packets of ingredients found in the apartment included castor beans, the raw material for ricin, one of the most easily made and yet effective poisons of all, which makes it an ideal resource for terrorists. The police also discovered apple seeds and ground cherry-stones from which cyanide can be extracted. Cyanide is an extremely deadly substance that was used in the Nazi death camps during the World War II (although vast amounts of apple seeds and cherry stones are needed to provide a lethal quantity). The searchers also found acetone, which forms part of the chemical process used to extract poison from seeds, and equipment used to convert liquid poison into gas. Nicotine poison was discovered in a jar. There were copies of instructions on how to use everyday household items to make explosives, such as flash and smoke bombs, and the detonators to go with them. Diagrams of circuits suitable for detonators and improvised bombs commonly used by terrorists throughout the world were also lying around in the apartment. Most of the material was available on the internet. Some of the professional chemist's basic tools were there, including a pestle and mortar, coffee grinder, rubber gloves, blotting paper filters, thermometers, retorts, flasks and funnels.

It soon became apparent that the apartment in Wood Green was a chemical weapons factory and the formulae, written in Arabic, were scientifically sound and had been photocopied at the Finsbury Park Mosque prior to distribution throughout the disaffected Muslim community. Bourgass had written the instructions and his fingerprints were found on them. When Mustapha Taleb was arrested, the Special Branch also found a CD-rom in his possession that extolled the benefits of bombing using modern technology. It included instructions on how to assemble and plant timing devices.

Much of what is known about Bourgass came from Mohamed Meguerba, who was arrested by Algerian police soon after he fled to that country after breaking the bail conditions imposed in Britain. He was taken for interrogation and soon started to provide details of the terrorist cells operating in London and Manchester and other activities taking place at Finsbury Park Mosque, as well as spilling the beans against Al Qaeda. Meguerba's confession and twenty-seven pages of statements, which were almost certainly extracted under torture, were immediately passed to the British Secret Service. He told his interrogators that he had been part of a group making home-made chemical weapons and planning attacks on individuals, "including Jews", on the British mainland. The objective was to spread alarm and fear. He said that the plans included smearing poison liquids and pastes on cars and door handles in North London. Meguerba claimed to have filled two jars with ricin that he had made and had handed the poison on to a man called Nadir at the apartment in Wood Green Lane. The police who raided the apartment discovered the plans, but there was no sign of the jars of ricin.

If you were going to clone an Islamic terrorist, you would probably fashion him to look and behave like Kamel Bourgass.

Bourgass had arrived in Dover from Calais in the back of a lorry in January 2000 and had travelled straight to the Finsbury Park Mosque, where he was told to claim asylum at the Immigration Centre in Croydon. During his first asylum application, in February 2000, he gave the name Nadir Habra and said that he had been born in 1973. He gave the mosque as his address and claimed that he had no passport. It took twenty months for his application to be processed and thrown out. His appeal against the decision was rejected in December 2001. Bourgass/Habra, correctly predicting the outcome, failed to turn up at the appeal, thereby avoiding arrest and deportation, and disappeared into the North London Muslim community.

On the run in the back streets of Tottenham and Edmonton, he changed his identity and acquired a false French passport. When, in July 2002, he was stopped by police, he claimed to be Kamel Bourgass, a Moroccan born in 1975. Anti-terrorist police and the Special Branch failed to identify him as Nadir Habra but did decide to take an interest in Bourgass and his associates. The apartment in Wood Green Lane was uncovered during a separate investigation into a European-wide fraud ring, which was understood to be raising funds for Al Qaeda.

The police made arrests throughout North London in September 2002, and picked up Mouloud Sihali, who specialized in arranging accommodation and identity papers for asylum seekers. Five false passports were unearthed in his apartment in Ilford, including one bearing the picture of a wanted terrorist suspect. The police also found details of an address in Thetford where they arrested David Khalef. Sihali and Khalef were convicted of passport offences but not charged under the Anti-Terrorism Act. However, in Khalef's briefcase they discovered papers in Arabic on which were printed instructions on how to manufacture poison and explosives. Scientists at Porton Down Research laboratories tested the poison instructions and confirmed that they could be used to make lethal doses of toxins. The discovery that there were immigrants in London with the knowledge and capability to make deadly poisons that could be used in an attack on the capital, had a major impact on the security forces, and suspects were kept under surveillance by MI5 for several months. Bourgass, now about to become the most wanted man in Britain, walked out of the apartment in Wood Green Lane just hours before police raided the premises. His fingerprints and passport photographs were found in the apartment and circulated to all police forces. But the police now had no idea where he was or, in fact, who he was. Bourgass made his way to Bournemouth, from where he decided to take the night coach from Weymouth to Manchester. He was in desperate need of a false passport and so he made his way to a safe house in Crumpsall Lane, a quiet street in the north of the city. It was the home of a Libyan, Kalid Alwerfeli. This was a disastrous mistake for Bourgass, as the police had already planned to raid the premises. The net was now closing in on him.

The discovery of the Wood Green Lane apartment had obviously been a major coup by the security services. It was the result of MI5 passing on a tip that it had received from anti-terrorist police in Paris. The building had been watched for some time and the men using it had been filmed and followed. However, while that raid appeared to be a significant setback for terrorism in Britain, the subsequent police operation in Manchester, known as "Operation Salt", was a disaster. At half past four on the afternoon of January 14, 2003, Flat 4, at Number 4, Crumpsall Lane was raided by Special Branch officers, immigration officials and a three-man Tactical Aid Unit (TAU), which specialize in breaking into and securing houses. It was the unit's job to force its way into the apartment. The main target of the raid, Sofiane Mihoubi, whose arrest had been ordered by the Home Secretary David Blunkett as the result of information passed on by MI5, was known to be in the apartment. The third occupant was Khalid Alwerfeli, the thirty-one-year-old Libyan who rented the apartment. In November 2002, Alwerfeli had been granted indefinite leave to remain in Britain. He was the only member of the cell who was not Algerian. He had entered the UK in 1999 using a forged French identity card.

The raid on Crumpsall Lane was planned immediately after the discovery of the poison and explosives in Wood Green Lane. The police and immigration officials involved had no idea of the peril they were in. In retrospect, their approach can only be described as casual. At the trial at the Old Bailey, Nigel Sweeney listed what he euphemistically described as "the Police short-comings" in the operation, which involved 23 officers. He told the court, "There was no risk assessment, no written operational orders, no advance reconnaissance of the premises to determine exactly where the apartment was, no knowledge of who was in the apartment, or even whether Bourgass was there, no secure operational briefing before the raid, no clarity about the operational roles of each officer, no general understanding of the significance of the targets, no arrest kits containing restraints, no properly planned communications and no body armour." The only operational briefing took place in a garage at Collyhurst Police Station, while shifts were being changed. Surveillance appears to have been cursory, probably because there was insufficient time to set it up and analyse the risks. To make matters worse, there was tension between the Special Branch officers involved in the raid and the chief inspector who was running the operation, and the Special Branch mobile phone network crashed during the raid, forcing the officers to use their own personal phones. To add to the failures, Mohamed Meguerba, a key player in the conspiracy, was arrested but then granted bail and was able to abscond to Algeria, where he was later arrested.

It would seem obvious to most people that when the target is a terrorist cell there is a need for extreme caution on the part of the police officers involved and that the priority must be to ensure that everyone found on the premises is immobilized as quickly as possible. But this was not carried out. The police subsequently said that Bourgass seemed quiet and that they had been keen not to disturb any scientific evidence on his hands and body. The police ordered the occupants to strip, and then placed their clothes in bags and gave the suspects white overalls to wear. The Special Branch officers were not wearing body armour and for ninety minutes after they entered the premises, Kamel Bourgass was not handcuffed. The plastic tie-ups that would normally have been used to bind a suspect's hands had been left behind at the police station.

Bourgass gave a false name to the police and immigration officials who entered the apartment, but he was recognized from photographs provided by the security services. The police knew that the incriminating documents found in Wood Green Lane had Bourgass's fingerprints all over them and that he was a major terrorist suspect. It was obvious that he was in a desperate situation and that his arrest would mean a lifetime in prison unless he found a way to escape. However, he was guarded in a bedroom by a uniformed Police Constable called Fleming who was serving on only his first terrorist operation with the TAU. Sofiane Mihoubi was also in the room and was sitting on the second bed, where he was guarded by Police Constable Stephen Oake. Alwerfeli was in the living room, under guard by two Special Branch men. There were more police and immigration officers on the landing outside the apartment and others in the sitting room, taking photographs and gathering evidence.

Bourgass had remained passive, offering no resistance. He was waiting until he felt that his captors were relaxed and had lost their edge. He is a strong, wiry, well-built man and had the advantages of surprise, desperation and better knowledge of his surroundings. It was 5.45pm when, without warning, Bourgass rose from the bed, struck Constable Fleming hard in the groin, ran to the kitchen, picked up a knife with a 12cm blade from the draining board and began stabbing everyone within his reach. "He was prepared to murder anyone who got in his way," said Nigel Sweeney at the trial. During the struggle, Police Constable Oake, a father of three children and a lay preacher in his spare time, was stabbed four times in the chest. Three of the blows were fatal. One thrust penetrated his heart and two other blows penetrated his lungs. Two other Special Branch officers were wounded during the attack. One was stabbed twice in the arm and another unnamed detective, named in court only as John, was stabbed in the chest, side and back. Sergeant Paul Grindrod from the TAU was stabbed in the back and leg. Bourgass managed to land a total of thirteen blows during his frenzied attack.

The terrible consequence of the discovery of the terrorist bomb factory was not only the death of Stephen Oake, but was the realization that the British security services are not trained or yet capable of dealing with committed terrorists, even those as incompetent as Bourgass. Although all the information of a terrorist threat was available to the police and security services, they lacked the capability to analyse it and make constructive use of it in a way that would allow them to arrest all the suspects speedily and efficiently. Bourgass was a failed asylum seeker, an illegal immigrant, and was clearly an unstable and dangerous man. Even though he was caught, convicted and jailed, the very fact that he spent a number of years moving freely about Britain and Europe must have given encouragement to other extremists already in Britain. There is evidence that Bourgass was, in fact, a member of a cell of terrorists led by an Algerian, Abu Doha. During 1998, Doha, also known as "The Doctor", "Rachid" and "Amar Makhulif", was known to run a network of such cells. He was reputedly a member of the "Salafist Group for Call and Combat" which has committed widespread atrocities in Algeria and had been commissioned to establish the Khalden Training Camp in Afghanistan, where North Africans and Mujahadin members were trained. The camp processed hundreds of terrorists and Osama Bin Laden was a regular visitor, according to some who trained there and have since been arrested. Many were sent to fight in Chechnya, and others were sent to operate undercover in the West.

Doha established himself in North London where there is a strong Algerian community, made up of those escaping from the bitter fighting in their homeland. According to Mr Justice Ouseley, when sentencing one of Doha's associates, "His presence, like that of Bourgass, added cohesion to the Algerian Extremist cause in Britain." At the end of 2000, as a result of a tip-off from MI6 officers, who had intercepted a phone call from Doha, German police raided an address in Frankfurt where they discovered four men, along with bomb-making equipment and a surveillance video of Strasbourg Market. Three of the men in the apartment were British. All were arrested and subsequently jailed. Doha, travelling on a false passport, was arrested at Heathrow in February 2001 as he tried to catch a flight to Saudi Arabia. His apartment in Edmonton turned out to be a rich source of incriminating material including bomb-making instructions and false passports. He remains in custody in Belmarsh prison and is fighting extradition to the US. No one seems to know whether Doha's network of terrorists continues or whether it is finished with Bourgass' arrest. Activists in the Al Qaeda camps are trained to be self-sufficient and to continue without other members of the cadre when necessary.

Convicted terrorist Ahmed Ressam, who is in jail in the US after plotting a bomb attack on Los Angeles Airport, was in close contact with Doha before his arrest. Ressam was picked up in Seattle carrying arms and explosives for use in the attack. With the threat of a 130-year prison sentence hanging over him, he has since decided to co-operate with the FBI. Djamel Beghal, from Leicester, another member of the cell, was arrested in Dubai in 2001 and charged with a plot to attack the US embassy in Paris. He remains in a French Prison. A former Tunisian professional footballer, Nizar Trabelsi, who had also trained with Doha in Afghanistan, was arrested in Brussels with bomb-making equipment, having apparently volunteered as a suicide bomber. He had plotted to bomb the NATO Kleine Brogel military airbase. Many of the suspected members of Doha's network were rounded up after the Emergency Powers Act was introduced in 2001. Its new head, Kadre, was arrested in London, on his way, police believe, to activating Bourgass and helping in the ricin plot. Bourgass was picked up two months later and his detention probably marks the end of that cell. In retrospect, the plan to use ricin and the disgusting sounding "rotten meat poison" sounds eccentric, but the fact is that it could have happened and would certainly have created dreadful panic in the capital. It would also have increased tension between law-abiding Muslims and the communities in which they live.

The Bourgass trial poses some difficult questions for MI5 and, especially, for the Immigration Service. For years, French intelligence agencies had been warning the British Security Services that Algerians implicated in atrocities within their home country and elsewhere had been slipping into Britain and claiming asylum. But little was done about the information. British authorities justified their inaction by saying that they had no evidence of lawbreaking. The attack on the Twin Towers and the new anti-terrorist legislation naturally changed all that and concentrated the minds of the security services. From then on, French intelligence was given more credence and a permanent watch was, apparently, kept on the Algerian community. It has to be said, however, that the "watch" was not very satisfactory. In spite of what had been said, Bourgass was able to come and go as he pleased, travelling to Europe on false papers and constantly changing his identity without coming to the notice of the authorities. The claimed increase in surveillance had little impact and the Immigration Service showed appalling laxity. The Finsbury Park Mosque, long suspected as being a cover for illegal immigrants and for supplying false identity documents, seems to have been completely ignored and did not come under investigation until it was almost too late. The Algerians with whom Bourgass mixed were not stopped at any of the ports and airports that they travelled through. There are about a hundred million entries into the United Kingdom every year and obviously only a small number are terrorists. Nevertheless, there are very few immigration staff available to check who is passing through and to deal with any suspicious visitors. It seems hard to believe now, but in 2002 there were no immigration enforcement officers on duty in London at all after five o'clock in the afternoon.

The Americans, with their porous borders to the north, south and east, have been fighting illegal immigration on this scale for many more years than the British. Any scheme that is to have any hope of keeping undesirables out of the country has to be able to deal with the policing of its massive coastlines and borders – as well as its airspace. September 11 prompted a nationwide call for border security to be tightened up and, most importantly, for an answer to the question, "How do we stop more attacks?" The first decision taken, which was made in the immediate aftermath of the disaster, was that all commercial aircraft still in flight were to be grounded at the nearest airport, so that the enemy would be denied the use of the skies. This made operational sense as the skies were then full of heavily armed military aircraft at the time, and there was a great risk that an innocent airliner might be shot down by a jumpy trigger-happy fighter pilot. But this decision meant that air travel was also being denied to all law-abiding citizens of the United States. If you shut down your air traffic network, it is tantamount to admitting that you cannot defend it, which does more damage to the standing of the country than even the terrorists has brought about. During 2002 alone there were 8,789,123 civil airline departures in the United States – that is an average of over 24,000 flights a day. A total of 539,811,008 passengers checked into US airports in 2002, amounting to nearly one and a half million passengers every single day that year. Air travel is a huge and vital industry in the US, relying on hundreds of commercial airports. Clearly it is impossible to prevent all penetration of airport perimeter fences without severely restricting the daily flow of air traffic.

The Bush administration was well aware of the United States' vulnerability to attack and how quickly its transport network can be brought to a standstill. There are dozens of targets which, if attacked and seriously damaged, would quickly leave the nation crippled. For instance, the Mississippi river runs from Minnesota to the Gulf of Mexico and is, of course, criss-crossed by a large number of bridges. The heaviest road and rail traffic, however, is confined to around two dozen crossings. If just six of these crossings were taken out of action, east–west road and rail traffic would suffer huge delays and the US economy would be paralysed. A similar problem exists in Manhattan, which on an average week day, has a working population of around three million people. There are only six bridges and four tunnels to get you on and off the island. A chemical or biological attack could leave the island isolated, creating massive public panic; result in the failure of the US broadcasting and financial systems; and cause national despair. Severe damage to the oil industry could be achieved simply by blocking the Houston Ship Canal, along which oil is carried by ship from the Gulf of Mexico to feed the refineries in Pasadena. A scuttled supertanker would bring about an immediate oil shortage in the US. Advanced, industrial countries are always vulnerable to a bomb in a power station, ship or government building. After the destruction of the Twin Towers, there was little the administration could do other than warn of possible future attacks and demand tough legislation.

Immediately after the attack on the Twin Towers, security and immigration services were given the task of creating a new passenger screening programme to try to prevent such an outrage happening again. The identification of a small number of potential terrorists out of the ten million passenger movements taking place every day requires mountains of data from which potential terrorists must be identified and separated from the overwhelming bulk of people who pose no threat to the state. It has to be designed as a permanent programme that would examine every passenger reservation electronically in and out of all United States civil airports, authenticate the travellers, and create a profile of each person travelling. Anomalies or profiles that fall foul of the criteria set down by the intelligence agencies would be checked to decide whether on not the individuals identified might belong to terrorist organizations. It is a massive – and a potentially disastrous – plan.

The programme, CAPPS11, was so sensitive and secret that it had to be discreetly and temporarily dropped during the 2004 Presidential elections. The key to CAPPS11 was the involvement of companies like the Acxiom Corporation, a credit-ratings and data-sifting company that holds the details of virtually every individual in the US and Europe. Its partners, NC Software, specializes in risk detection and has developed software capable of the complex and detailed analysis of simple commercial transactions. These companies can process billions of records simultaneously and are experienced in working with the insurance industry, credit card issuers and telephone companies. They are experts at detecting fraud before and after it happens.

Much of the data-processing industry offered its services free to US law enforcement agencies while the Twin Towers were still burning. Within hours it was accepting requests for database analysis from the FBI, the Secret Service and the police. LexisNexis, which is sometimes mistaken for a legal resource or a cuttings agency, also offered immediate help. LexisNexis is actually a subsidiary of the giant British publishing business Reed Elsevier, which is based in London but has US subsidiaries. LexisNexis owns detailed records of millions of individuals, families and companies originally acquired from public records detailing social security numbers, dates of birth and much more. The company originally operated as a legal library for the US Internal Revenue Service and created a telecommunications system to help speed up the service the IRS provides for its customers. In the late nineties, LexisNexis acquired a business called Risk-Wise that automatically assesses reports for inconsistency and potential risk. LexisNexis was now able to allocate a "score" to individuals based on factors such as their suitability for employment or their experience or level of skill at a particular type of work. LexisNexis' capabilities were ideal for an administration attempting to work out the risk potential of another disaster like the one that had just befallen the US.

LexisNexis now owns 16,000 databases, has 3 million subscribers and uses 36,000 information sources such as public records, court decisions, business results, credit assessments and even word of mouth. It works for the intelligence services, the media and the legal profession. If you want to check that someone is suitable for work involving children, LexisNexis will provide you with a background portrait of the applicant, listing any criminal convictions and virtual anything else you want to know. The company's systems process and analyse information on millions of people in response to a wide variety of criteria. In the chaotic wake of the disaster in New York, LexisNexis agreed to established a "Downtown Disaster" Task Force in Washington DC and made its databases accessible to all law enforcement agencies. The atmosphere prevailing at the time was that everything possible should be done to catch the men behind the outrage and put them behind bars. This was not only out of a desire to avenge the atrocity but also because the authority and independence of the United States had to be protected at all costs. There was no limit to the co-operation that commerce was willing to provide. The data agencies knew that not only was their help vital but it was also an investment in goodwill that would pay dividends in the future. Overnight, professionally assembled information had become a priceless commodity. Clearly, for some, the tragedy of 9/11 had become a golden business opportunity.

The LexisNexis systems and computers were soon linked up to government computers and intelligence service databanks. Not surprisingly, one of the company's priorities was to use its risk-scoring technology as a means of analyzing the reliability of the identities claimed by non-US citizens applying for courses in flight training schools. The Bush administration had drawn up a list of over twenty thousand terrorist suspects, based on all sorts of questionable criteria, and LexisNexis was given the responsibility of monitoring them constantly. Most of the names on the list were completely innocent of any wrongdoing but the company's techniques achieved some notable successes and, for example, successfully identified the house in Florida that the hijack terrorists had shared while they went through their flight training.

LexisNexis was sensitive to US Government concerns about the fact that the company was British owned, and so laboriously went about the task of setting up a new subsidiary in 2003 called LexisNexis Special Service. This satisfied the government lawyers, secret services and law enforcement agencies, as well as the Bush administration itself, and the company was immediately given clearance to handle the United States' most sensitive secrets. The new company became responsible for the Aviation Security Project, CAPPS11, which it started to develop with a new government agency called The Office of National Risk Assessment. It was at this stage that LexisNexis started to charge for its work.

In 2003, the civil liberties organizations began to hear the first stories about CAPPS11 and the concept of applying threat risk assessments to every air carrier, passenger, airport and flight made in the US as well as to every passenger flying in and out of the US. A group called Electronic Privacy Information Centre (EPIC) became extremely agitated about what it was hearing. It seems astonishing now that the State Department or the Department of Homeland Security had omitted to share any information with the civil rights pressure groups or the media about CAPPS11 system, because this was a story that was bound to leak out eventually, and when it did, the response would be exponentially ferocious. And that was exactly what happened. The Government was discovered in the act of setting up the largest domestic surveillance systems ever imposed on the American public, without disclosing any details to the organizations that would be most concerned about it.

David Sobel, general counsel at EPIC, immediately opposed the concept of what amounted to "government identities" for anyone wishing to travel. Other proposals soon became apparent too, including the use of x-ray cameras and state-sponsored profiling. Sobell and other campaigners protested on the simple grounds that any database as massive and flexible as CAPPS11 would be inaccurate. He made the point that the FBI accepted that its criminal records database had an inaccuracy level of 33 per cent. As the CAPPS11 system was steadily introduced, the US government created a "no fly selectee list" and began to enforce it. Gradually, stories began to emerge that more and more respectable people were being stopped at airport check-in desks and refused permission to fly. There had always been lists like this, in the UK as well as the US, but none of the individuals whose names were being circulated to airline offices and airports all over the country were being told why they were being singled out. The lists of names supplied by the intelligence community and the Department of Homeland Security seemed to grow every day. Often the people concerned appeared to have Arab or Asian names, but there was rarely any further explanation. Any attempt to challenge the classification of "someone who is not permitted to fly" was immediately rejected. Experts involved with CAPPS11 soon became concerned about the project too, which was why it was discreetly halted in the run-up to the 2004 Presidential elections. Now, it has been resurrected. Simon Davies, of the pressure group Privacy International, described it as a "disaster waiting to happen". He said, "There will be miscarriages of justice and we know from experience that there will be chaos on an unprecedented scale in the country's airports."

Maybe CAPPS11 is the future? The only satisfactory way of establishing our true credentials may eventually be to have a chip embedded beneath our skin, probably at birth.

Chapter Ten: How the Europeans Do It

Since the Iraq War, there has been a noticeable widening in the political gulf between Europe and the US. The French not only declined to become involved in the Iraq War, they also gained huge political capital out of the stance they took and antagonized the Americans in the process. Despite the 2004 Madrid railway bombing, in neighbouring Spain, there seems to be little fear of terrorist violence among the French people. If you visit Paris or Lyons, you will find that these cities too have their crime and immigration difficulties, yet somehow public surveillance is not so intrusive as it is in the UK. In contrast, the British authorities have developed an uninhibited attitude towards surveillance and the UK has now become the most watched country in the world. We have a long legacy of terrorist activity in the British Isles and any signs hinting at a change in IRA behaviour have swiftly brought about an increase in state surveillance and intelligence gathering. We tend to accept this situation almost without complaint, perhaps believing that, one day the terrorist problem will go away and the world will return to normal.

But what about our European neighbours? For years, the Dutch have been the most liberal of peoples, yet all that changed when Pim Fortuyn was killed. Germany suffered under the hands of the Bader Meinhof group, but the country seems to have other problems on its hands, and terrorism comes a little further down the list. So what is happening in Europe?

Since the Iraq War the deepening anti-American feeling in France seems to have strengthened the country's demand for freedom and privacy, in spite of its inherent conservatism. There is little public video surveillance in France and Germany, once you are away from the French autoroutes and the German autobahns. Crime hotspots in the town centres are sometimes monitored, but this is deeply unpopular and frequently leads to unrest and demonstrations. As soon as surveillance cameras are put in place, members of a French pressure group called Regardez Vous invariably turn up and paint the lenses black. The group has even been to New York and demonstrated in Times Square. The violence perpetrated against MacDonalds in Paris and in the provincial towns and cities is not only due to a perception by some French groups that these are intrusive American cultural symbols but also because of the burger company's habit of installing cameras to watch the customers and, occasionally, staff. French intransigence over the war in Iraq just made things worse.

The Americans decided to march into Iraq in 2003 assuming that other nations, especially their traditional allies such as France, would be happy to trade a little national autonomy in exchange for prosperity and stability. America, as the most powerful nation in the world, was demanding from other nations a clear recognition of its power and also tacit agreement that they agreed with the US view of the global political situation, following the end of the Cold War. The American mistake was to assume that automatic support would be forthcoming over the decision to go to war with Iraq. Choosing to be allies of America made perfect sense to many politicians on both sides of the political divide in the UK. After all, US military might is awesome and so it seems like a good idea to benefit from its protective umbrella. And, anyway, for a long time the deal has been, "help us and we will help you". There was, however, another consideration that weighed more heavily with the Europeans. America's strength was such that, when it came to foreign policy, the US had a huge choice of options from which to select, and this made the country unpredictable. You never knew what you would be drawn into or even if the US would one day turn against you. What France and Germany wanted was a more predictable and rational United States.

The US did not realize that, for almost a decade, its actions had been seen as hostile in countries such as France, Germany, Russia and China. The Islamic world, in particular, had taken a battering from the US in Somalia, Bosnia, Kosovo and Iraq. The interventions of the US, against what they saw as Al Qaeda's plans to create a trans-national Islamic state, simply allowed Muslim fundamentalist groups to label America as an enemy of Islam and so mobilize even more support. Al Qaeda was born as a result of Desert Storm, the US-led invasion of Iraq in 1990, and the group had prospered ever since. So there was now opposition to the war against Iraq, not only from the Islamic world but also from America's old Cold War allies.

To the French, the rise of American power has been seen as a threat to France's economic and strategic interests in the Middle East, so knocking the US down to size became part of French foreign policy. France was committed to the idea of a united Europe acting as a counterbalance to the United States, with France and Germany together controlling Europe. European opposition to America would help lift the EC up from being a solely economic community to becoming a major global political power. There has been a residue of anti-American feeling in France since World War I. The French President, Jacques Chirac, believed in 2003 that this feeling had also spread throughout other countries of the European Union. President Bush miscalculated, expecting the French to hesitate and argue before finally agreeing to support the cause and say "yes" to his plans to unseat Saddam Hussein and create a democracy in Iraq. The CIA reported that the French agreed with the British and American belief that Iraq had weapons of mass destruction and was prepared to use them. Consequently the Bush administration expected the French to agree with the US position, or be forced to stand up in the UN and explain why the country was prepared to tolerate weapons of mass destruction in the hands of Saddam.

The United States failed to understand that France saw the American decision to invade as the ideal opportunity to galvanize Europe under French leadership. Nor did the US understand the extent of France's concern that the rise of American power was threatening European and French interests in the Middle East. The US also believed it had an arrangement with France that would bring the two countries together if and when Iraq refused to allow UN weapons inspectors to enter the country in November 2002. However, President Chirac had no intention of agreeing to this and against a background of overwhelmingly anti-war opinion polls throughout Europe, was working toward the creation of an anti-war coalition. In January, France, Germany and Russia all rejected a UN resolution to authorize war against Iraq.

US Defense Secretary Donald Rumsfeld made a speech in which he described the French and the Germans as "Old Europe". It sounded like a tactical blunder, but it was conceived as a means of isolating Germany and France from the rest of Europe because of the growing fear of a Franco-German axis dominating European foreign policy. Toward the end of the twentieth century, France had started to build an ambitious and provocative satellite surveillance system designed to collect intelligence. It is run along similar lines to that of Echelon, the global surveillance program run by Britain and America. Echelon is based on a fleet of military satellites and listening stations all over the globe, and has developed into the world's biggest intelligence gathering system. Now there are clear signs that, through France and her Helios satellites, European countries have an international surveillance system of their own.

France has three spy satellites in orbit, all working in conjunction with a network of listening stations that together systematically monitor, gather and transmit communications in the United States and elsewhere. Monitoring stations are known to have been built in French Guiana, the city of Domme in the Dordogne region of south-west France, New Caledonia in the South Pacific and the United Arab Emirates. The French monitoring stations in New Caledonia and the United Arab Emirates are used to capture satellite transmissions in space, and to cover transmissions in Asia and the Middle East. The listening posts in the Caribbean are used to intercept conversations in the United States.

It is not an exclusively military system and, as is the case with Echelon, the data that is gleaned is sent to both military and commercial markets. The French project is the first step in a Europe-wide attempt to compete with the global spying activities of the US. The French project is operated by the Direction Générale de la Sécurité Extérieure, a spying and surveillance agency, set up in a similar way to the CIA. The French DGSE has also entered into an agreement with Germany's foreign intelligence agency Bundesnachrichtendienst (BND) to share information mined from their Helios programme in return for partial funding of the project. Commercial information is transmitted directly to the chief executives of the contributing French and German companies, as well as to the French Intelligence services. The existence of a global surveillance capability has never been officially confirmed or denied by the French Government, although its existence is generally accepted among the French public and is common knowledge among the international intelligence community.

Unlike Echelon and the US listening station at Menwith Hill, whose existence is also common knowledge throughout the UK and Europe, there is little official evidence that France or any other European nation practices systematic surveillance of international civilian and military communications. It is one of those subjects that is never commented on. British officials who are familiar with the French system admit privately that it exists, but say it is considerably smaller than Echelon. The French newspaper *Le Point*, in a report on French intelligence gathering, quoted a government official as saying that while Echelon intercepts around three million messages per minute, the French system intercepts roughly two million messages per month. But the truth is that no one really knows and the Direction Générale de la Sécurité Extérieure (the official in charge of external security who was quoted) is understandably being "economical avec l'actualite" (economical with the truth). What is known is that the French have updated their satellite spy facilities since this report was made, and that they will continue to do so.

However, France has at least admitted to developing an international surveillance capability. François Roussely, the chief of staff at the French Ministry of Defence, has admitted that the system is used for monitoring international crises that are of concern to the French military, as well as combating terrorism and preventing the spread of non-conventional weapons. France has close intelligence ties with its neighbours the UK, Germany, Spain and Italy. It would be madness if it didn't. The Sécurité Extérieure was in close contact with MI5 during the trial of the Algerian terrorist Bourgass and has links with the vice and people-smuggling units of the Metropolitan Police. France is a conduit for criminals who travel to the west coast of Europe from Africa, and through the Balkans into Europe. The fact is that Europe is gradually becoming a spying and intelligence unit with power and resources to rival that of the US.

Communication intercepts by the DGSE do not fall under the laws governing French wiretapping, which require that tapped individuals must be criminal suspects, according to the Commission Nationale de Contrôle des Interceptions de Sécurité. The objectives of French surveillance is almost certainly more far reaching. Wiretaps, as practised by the DGSE do not necessarily have to be linked to the objective of preventing normal criminal activity.

The French system is believed to target the Intelsat and Inmarsat civilian communications satellites, among others. The satellites used in the French surveillance project are the Hélios series in a programme called Euracom. However, the original satellites launched in the late 1990s are said to be showing their age and have comparatively poor technical capacity for inter-ception and re-transmission. As a consequence, the French have reportedly begun an experimental initiative called "Cerise" to intercept satellite communications. They recently launched a new and far more efficient Helios military surveillance satel-lite, the 2A. It is designed and built in France and has far greater power and capability than either of its predecessors.

The latest Helios 2A was launched into orbit by a European Ariane rocket in 2004. The 2A is the first of a new generation of spy satellites launched by France. It weighs over 4 tonnes and was built by an industrial consortium led by EADS-Astrium. According to the French, it is designed to mark the start of European challenge to the United States domination of NATO intelligence gathering. The Ariane-5 rocket blasted off from the European Space Agency (ESA) launch site in French Guiana on the north-east coast of South America. An hour after lift-off, the Helios 2A separated from the rocket and then a further six "micro-satellites" were released from the rocket.

France's Defence Minister Michele Alliot-Marie has said, "In Europe, we talk about the four freedoms of the Union – freedom for the flow of information, of the mobility of people, freedom of goods and freedom of services, but there is a fifthfreedom, which is intelligence. Nations want to retain the freedom to spy." She called for greater European co-operation in space defence initiatives. "With Helios, French military capability can benefit from the increased capacity, more accurate and rapid reaction capacity. The status of being a power in space has become essential to exist on the world stage." Earlier generation Helios 1 satellites launched aboard Ariane rockets in 1995 and 1999 were technically less sophisticated and will soon be replaced. Lieutenant Colonel Inaky Garcia Brotons of the French Air Force, told the Reuters news agency before the launch, "This satellite is considerably more sophisticated. The infra-red system gives us much more accurate detection of human activity. For instance, in bad visibility or at night, it can tell whether a truck convoy is moving or halted, or whether a nuclear reactor is operational or not."

French defence officials said that although the Helios 2 generation would be capable of operating at night they could not capture images through thick cloud. The total cost of the programme, including a second satellite to be launched in three years' time, was two billion euros ($2.6 billion), with France foot-ing 95 per cent of the financing. The French are remarkably ret-icent about their fleet of surveillance satellites and their plans to invest in more military surveillance hardware in space. Despite a growing chorus of disapproval from French civil lib-erties groups, there seems to be no reliable information avail-able concerning the regularity of possible interceptions, specific targets, or the volume of traffic.

According to a published account from the *Journal Officiel de la République Française*, the government's daily legislative and regulatory record, agreements exist between the French and German intelligence agencies to share the cost of global satellite surveillance. In a question to the Prime Minister's office concerning intelligence operations, Nicolas About, a French Deputy, said, in a particularly creepy statement, "We congratu-late the resources the government has committed under the law covering military operations for the recruitment in this intelligence service and their operational ability with the Franco-German programme of satellite surveillance." If this statement does nothing else, it seems to confirm that the two governments are now co-operating on military satellites that are more than capable of spying on the French populations as well as Islamic extremists in Algeria. The Helios satellites are used for photographic reconnaissance, and the surveillance data is shared with intelligence agencies in Germany, Spain and Italy.

There are obvious financial constraints on this type of technology, but that is not the sole reason for investing in this kind of programme and broadening it to involve European allies. German financial involvement in the system helps explain why the Bush administration has been unsuccessful, despite long-running efforts, in persuading Bonn to reject French military satellites and accept US help in building German intelligence-gathering capabilities. The French have recently invested in four E-3 Airborne Warning and Control System (AWACS). The AWACS was selected to meet the primary airborne early warning requirements of the French Republic. This aircraft is the world's standard for airborne early warning, the E-3 was designed and delivered by Boeing and the four French Air Force E-3s perform both airborne surveillance, and command and control functions. They carry surveillance enhancements that have been added to meet French unique mission requirements and have a powerful capability to intercept and transmit signals from ground or satellite sources. They use a probe refuelling system to augment the existing boom receptacle for in-flight refuelling, a digital recorder for mission audio transmissions and improved radio equipment. According to an RAF source, the French early warning and AWACS surveillance ESM is a passive listening and detection system, which enables the AWACS to detect, identify and track electronic transmissions from ground, airborne and maritime sources. Using the ESM system, mission operators are able to determine radar and weapons system type. A major element of direct support was French installation of the E-3 mission equipment. Boeing delivered the aircraft empty to Le Bourget airport near Paris, where the French systems were installed.

The inevitable fact is that in Europe and the United States, government and industry all admit that "friendly spying" for political and economic reasons is widespread among Western allies. In other words, surveillance, industrial espionage, stealing secrets and eavesdropping may not be acceptable in a civilized society, but go on anyway. The European Parliament's annual STOA report details US surveillance operations, yet the US has become outraged at the thought that its space is being invaded and its communications network is being spied on. The US accuses European nations, and other countries, of "spying and global intelligence gathering," which includes listening in to US citizens and companies.

The US National Counterintelligence Center (NACIC) in its annual report says that "foreign governments conducting industrial espionage", is a real and major concern, although no specific countries were publicly named. "A number of foreign countries pose various levels and types of threats to US economic and technological information. Most of the countries concerned are either long-time allies of the United States or have traditionally been neutral. They have started to target and capture US economic and technological information despite their friendly relations with the US."

France is without doubt one of the most active intelligence gatherers in the world, and sees itself as leading Europe in demonstrating European strength. The theft of industrial and commercial intelligence is not usually as sophisticated as many of us might expect and there is a wide range of options available to those involved in gathering information that might give them a financial edge in business dealings. For instance, there is straightforward telecommunications targeting and interception. Most lucrative of all, there is a slackness over secret coding (encryption) in the private sector that makes it easy to acquire vast amounts of data. The French admit that these techniques account for the largest portion of economic and industrial information obtained from US corporations.

Government-owned telecom businesses are another traditional target for state surveillance and espionage, and the targeting of bulk computer data transmissions and electronic mail and fax traffic is a priority, because they are easily accessed and intercepted. Corporate telecommunications, particularly international telecommunications, also provide a highly vulnerable and lucrative source of intelligence, according to unofficial sources within the NACIC.

There are regular allegations from within the US intelligence community about foreign nations that practice economic espionage against US firms. The FBI regularly identifies France, Germany, Israel, China, Russia and South Korea as the major culprits. This obvious and generally unnecessary revelation, typical of the Bureau, was made by Edwin Fraumann, a New York-based FBI agent, who wrote an academic analysis on international commercial espionage in *Public Administration Review*, published by the American Society for Public Administration. Fraumann alleged that French intelligence agents even wiretap US businessmen flying on the national airline, Air France, as well as intercepting telephone conversations and fax communications in hotels in France. The analysis went on to accuse Germany of operating a surveillance post near Frankfurt that is responsible for monitoring US phone conversations and of attempting to penetrate American computer systems. Compared to Echelon, this is, of course, small beer. But there is little doubt that French wiretapping and surveillance on a select group of visitors, particularly from America, is constant and professional.

There is certainly no doubt that Echelon collects huge amounts of confidential data on European business. American outrage is consequently misplaced and only expressed as part of a propaganda process. Bernd Schmidbauer, the director of German intelligence, denied the FBI's accusations in an article and stated that foreign espionage against German firms was a serious and costly problem. In turn, France and the European Parliament have criticized US global surveillance operations, and have shown reluctance to co-operate in cross-boarder intelligence operations with the United States because of a risk that it may entail a loss of privacy for citizens and encourage espionage against European companies. French government officials confirmed that the country had decided to change its cryptography policy in January 1999 and now encourages the use of encryption because of the sophistication of US interception capabilities. French Foreign Minister Hubert Védrine said in November 1998 that counterbalancing the threat posed by Echelon has become a "preoccupation" for the French government. In fact, both France and the US have long mistrusted each other on intelligence matters and an escalation of the problem dates from the Cold War period where France forged a "Third Way" policy of rapprochement with the USSR. In the early 1990s, France rejected an initiative by the FBI to co-operate on an international database of terrorists, simply because the programme was led by the US.

"Friendly spying" is a euphemism for behaviour likely to raise the diplomatic temperature. There have been many reported incidents of commercial and diplomatic espionage between friendly Western nations that have led to tension between Europe and the US. In December 1995, five US Embassy personnel were expelled from France after they were accused of being agents of the CIA. It was a strangely public incident, with deep political overtones, that occurred during a French presidential election campaign, and which led a senior US intelligence agent to state (to *The Washington Post*) that it would damage US-French intelligence co-operation for years to come. It was little more than a typically French political gesture that was intended to win votes. But the Americans have never forgotten it. As a further riposte to US criticism of Europe, a US citizen was deported from Germany in March 1997 for attempting to bribe an official at Germany's Economics Ministry.

Co-operation with the US in Europe is not necessarily always a good political move because of internal tensions that are inevitably created by allegations of joint European-US surveillance initiatives. Many MEPs and officials at the European Commission are reluctant to accept any sort of accord among European police agencies for co-operation in interception activities. The reason is that many European politicians see this as just another way of strengthening involvement with the FBI or the CIA. The European Council of Minister's "Resolution on the Legal Interception of Telecommunications in the Framework of New Technologies" was reputedly drafted with the help of the FBI, and the British-based civil liberties group Statewatch has produced what purports to be a confidential council working paper stating that the FBI participated in drafting the resolution as an "expert group" concerning the technical requirements for interception.

Nobody seems to be prepared to confirm that the Counsel Resolution on Police Eavesdropping (ENFOPOL 98) was intended for law enforcement purposes only, or is intended to enable wholesale interception of communications. There have been calls in Europe for intelligence co-operation throughout the EC, specifically in a working document of the West European Union, Europe's military alliance, entitled "A European Policy on Intelligence". Such a programme would involve information-gathering in areas outside of those regarded as traditional national security concerns. It is obvious that if the EU prospers and establishes itself as a world military power, then it must have an intelligence capability to support it. Intelligence has changed dramatically in recent years. It was always essentially a military matter, which depended to a great extent on human intelligence ("Humint") as its source. While it still has a military use, modern intelligence nearly always has a political, commercial and religious element as well.

All European governments are wary of the United States' surveillance capability, a state of mind that naturally makes any transatlantic intelligence co-operation difficult to forge. While the UK co-operated with the US totally during and after the Iraq War, surveillance in Europe became a matter for Europe alone, and continues to be so. The political and economic unity that was strengthened by the creation of a single currency may be extended to other areas, such as a joint European approach to surveillance technologies, which France will no doubt seek to spearhead.

As a result, rather than the creation of a single global surveillance system by Europe and the US, if France and Germany have their way, Europe will eventually establish its own independent project and compete with the US. A Europe-wide independent spy and surveillance network will not make privacy advocates sleep more easily in their beds at night safe in the knowledge that civil liberties are being protected. All that will happen is that the world will find itself with two powerful and intrusive surveillance systems instead of only one.

It is obvious that France now has the resources of a global surveillance technology and is using it. Thus it may serve as the start of a wider European initiative for intelligence gathering, which will mean that it is likely to exist outside of well-established national laws that are designed to protect privacy. In both the political and commercial arenas, Europe has strengthened its information security with encryption technology and electronic monitoring in order to protect against possible US interception of communications. The motivation for Europe's drive to invest in and develop surveillance technology is obviously to counterbalance US technical know-how. A major difficulty is that the US, in its struggle against the threat of global terror, requires immediate access to intelligence relating to terrorists. It is in no country's interest to deny them this, which means that relations at an operational level must continue to exist between the US and every country in Europe. For instance, after the Madrid bombings in March 2004, new evidence of the way Islamic terrorists evade detection by operating in loosely connected networks emerged from an investigation by intelligence sources in Paris and Madrid. Eleven days after the atrocity in the Spanish capital, the political associations that came to light between a key suspect in the bombing and Islamic militants elsewhere in Europe and North Africa were proof of a widening web of terror groups that may have had few direct links to Al Qaeda but were intent on achieving the same goals. The attack has revealed "an accumulation of strata from different networks that had been damaged but which managed to fuse together a collection of leftovers that regenerated itself", says Jean-Charles Brisard, a former French secret service agent, who is investigating Al Qaeda for lawyers representing relatives of the 9/11 victims.

"The regeneration of terrorist groups illustrates how the threat of terrorism has shifted from Al Qaeda to associated organizations inspired by bin Laden without necessarily waiting for his orders," says Dr Rohan Gunaratna, who wrote *Inside Al Qaeda: Global Network of Terror*. "It shows that Al Qaeda has become a movement, it is no longer a single group." Every time there is an atrocity, wherever it is, the US learns more about the enemy it has decided to pursue so remorselessly. The key, says Dr Gunaratna, is closer international co-operation among intelligence services. "European security services still look at terrorist networks as national problems," he says. "They have not matched the integration Al Qaeda has achieved in combining networks." America has, however.

Of course, there are civil liberties groups who see conspiracies everywhere intent on depriving us of our rights to privacy, particularly when the discussion turns to co-operation between the American intelligence community and Europe. It is understandable that this makes everyone nervous. Civil rights are a big deal in Paris and Bonn, and the European Parliament takes incursion into Europe from outside intelligence agencies like the FBI and CIA with understandably bad grace. Regular, and always rebuffed, demands from Brussels about what is going on at Menwith Hill do not help. It is understandable that France and Germany want their own capability in this field.

The Intelligence stand-off comes alongside a trend toward inter-governmental co-operation on law enforcement, such as efforts by the world's richest countries, the Group of Eight, and its "Lyon Group" to combat high-tech crime, or the Wassenaar Agreement to control the export of encryption technology.

While these international discussions continue, the surveillance activities aimed against citizens and companies of allied nations for purposes outside of traditional national security continue. The German government has approved a surveillance regulation intended to make it easier for the authorities to eavesdrop on communications via fixed-line and mobile phone, email, fax and SMS (short message service). The new law requires network providers to install and maintain equipment and procedures that give access to their customers' electronic traffic once the authorities have acquired a legal surveillance order. Eavesdropping "in cases of suspicion of certain serious crimes" is already allowed under existing law, apparently.

The regulations do not apply to private telephone companies and the technical requirements are limited to providers of "public telecommunication systems", which includes land-line and mobile phone operators and providers of email accounts, but not internet service providers (ISPs). Operators of the means of transmission that provide immediate user access to the internet, such as DSL (digital subscriber line) connections, are also required to install the eavesdropping technology. In Germany, the largest such operator is Deutsche Telekom AG, the former incumbent telecom provider, which is still majority-owned by the State. The German government says that the eavesdropping proposals were already on the table before 9/11, but there had been heavy criticism from the IT and telecoms industries, which complained of the high cost of installing the necessary technology. Of course, 9/11 changed all that and the industry has finally agreed to a compromise.

Naturally, not all industrial concerns were satisfied by the new law, according to the IT industry association BITKOM (Bundesverband Informationswirtschaft, Telekommunikation und neue Medien eV), but the regulation now apparently presents an acceptable compromise between the interests of the state in surveillance of telecommunication and unfettered use of the internet. The original plan would have involved the wholesale surveillance of service providers, but the compromise agreed by the German government focuses on user-network connections, which the industry say lightens the load for smaller network providers and ISPs.

Of course, the civil liberty organizations have not been so easily pacified. Twelve human rights groups made a joint statement warning of the danger of a "surveillance state" and citing the country's experiences with totalitarianism under the Nazi regime and East German Communism. "The balance between legally guaranteed citizen freedoms and the State's rights of encroachment must not be abolished in the interest of abstract state security." The groups, who are strong in Germany and taken very seriously there, include the Humanist Union, the German Association for Data Protection, and the hackers' group Chaos Computer Club. They claimed to be addressing not only the eavesdropping rule, but other proposed security measures including fingerprinting, the release of student records to police, and increased surveillance of foreigners.

It can be argued that the Germans were just bringing the protection of their citizens into line with everyone else. The US and the UK permit wiretapping, and France has passed laws that allow "decryption, under certain circumstances, of encrypted messages transmitted by means of the internet". The civil liberties groups retorted, "Almost all of the proposed measures massively interfere with basic rights. But none of them creates more security for citizens." A spokesman for the German Government said, "If you have nothing to hide, there's nothing to worry about." Where have we heard that before?

Chapter Eleven: Don't Vote For It

The 2005 British general election was a peculiarly unsatisfactory affair. The debates seemed narrow and banal, without any real meat. The media seemed to concentrate on broken promises and the nastiness of the campaign management. However, it was a marketing man's delight! Huge budgets were spent in five or six weeks of frantic activity. Both major parties had big campaign teams who the press, with their obsession with celebrity culture, did their best to turn into the stories.

Most of the action seemed to be going on in marginal seats where a few "undecided" voters held the key to the overall result. Most of these seats were held New Labour. At the beginning of the election run-up, all the major political parties believed the battle would be won or lost in these key marginals. The election managers, who had to cram their plans into a few weeks, then had to identify the voters they wanted to approach and concentrate their messages on them as forcefully as possible. The most efficient way of doing this was by means of advertising and direct mail. They had the resources to target electors by telephone, post and by personal contact. But how do you decide on the message you want to send? Political messages are designed to appeal to individuals, families, communities. They respond to concerns about the environment, tax, immigration, and so on. But how do the party campaign teams discover exactly what will motivate a voter unless they know *everything* about him or her? Their obvious problem, you might think, is that nobody can know that much about an individual. But actually, that's not quite true. Given time and access to a few personal records, an experienced research analyst can paint a pretty good picture of what motivates individuals most. It's happening all the time.

The UK general election of 2005 will be remembered for what was not discussed rather than what was. Europe, for instance, seemed to be a forgotten subject; it was hardly ever mentioned, yet Britain's future in Europe, as determined by the referendum over the new EC Constitution, will be one of the most important political issues of modern times. Nobody in the Conservative Party really went for the jugular on the economy, or defence spending, or the countryside. These subjects may well have come up as local issues, but nationally, it seemed that the battlegrounds had been carefully delineated along narrow lines. It was an infuriating campaign in many ways. Speeches were delivered in tabloid language and slogans written by cynical spinmasters and PR people, and then parroted endlessly. The print media overdosed on the conflict, analyzing and profiling and condemning and generally scraping the barrel. But even the press seemed reluctant to tackle important issues other than immigration, past records, verbal *faux pas,* or polls. The political commentators, seemingly desperate to find something new to say, became more and more extreme. On the eve of the election, the once venerable *Times* of London printed a page on which the two main headlines read "HOWARD URGED TO STAY IF DEFEATED" and "CONSERVATIVE SUPPORT REACHES A RECORD LOW."

The detailed knowledge of a politician's background is

fundamentally important during an election. Tabloid journalism must be personal. As a reporter, you are supposed to apply the following test to a story: does it contain the "who, what, when, where and why"? The vital element is always "who?" The files in the Murdoch Press and Associated Newspapers databases contain information on the lives and peccadilloes of political, industrial, show business and just "natural-born" celebrities. But it is the executive editor's desk and the safe in his office where the real stuff is kept. When Paul Dacre's office was being redecorated and was left unlocked, the London Daily Mail staff helped themselves to trolleyloads of his secrets and sold them to the satirical magazine Private Eye, where a tasty selection still remains. The media partly exists to learn, publish and comment on secrets, and, like the secret services, it will bug and burgle its way anywhere in the world to get what it wants. The men and women whose names appear so frequently must wait to find out what is to be revealed about them next – and when. Of course, if they have sold their stories through an agent they will know precisely what is going to be published and when. Even then, rival newspapers will put out "spoilers". These are stories their reporters have managed to cobble together from the scraps of facts and half-truths they have been able to glean about the subject and the "sensational" event concerned. The intention of the "spoiler" story is to minimize the impact of the other newspaper's "exclusive revelations" in order to protect their sales. It is difficult to control events once a story has "legs".

When, during the 2005 election campaign, I asked the news editor of a national Sunday newspaper what he wanted more than anything in the world, he said, without hesitation, "Nude pictures of Sandra Howard". He meant, of course, nude pictures taken in the 1960s when Sandra Paul, as she then was, had a very successful modelling career. All sixties models seem to have stripped off in front of the camera at some time or another, usually for David Bailey. As far as the Sunday paper news editor was concerned, someone, somewhere had such pictures of Sandra, and he wanted them. I asked him whether, if they existed and he managed to buy them, he would publish them during the election. He hesitated and then said, "Just having them is probably enough." It obviously had nothing to do with "news".

Of all the intelligence gatherers, the media is probably the most remorseless. They have the dirt on everyone in politics – and the politicians know it. Fleet Street operates a complicated network of unwritten agreements and deals. Some arrangements are well known, such as that between the Prince of Wales and his family and the packs of hacks and paparazzi who follow them everywhere. The deal is – the Royals allow "limited access in return for privacy". The agreement frequently breaks down because of the desperate competitiveness of the newshound "pack", but, generally speaking, it works.

If you take it as read that powerful editors like Paul Dacre know much more than their papers are prepared to reveal, you have to ask yourself what are the implications of this. For instance, Dacre and his staff might know that Lord "A", a government minister, is cheating on his wife but chooses not to reveal it in his newspaper, and Lord "A" knows that Dacre knows about it – but doesn't know why Dacre is keeping quiet. Does the fact that Dacre owns the knowledge automatically bring pressure to bear on Lord "A"? Does the act of withholding such information in itself constitute a serious problem? Who takes the final decision to publish a story? The editor, the proprietor – or whom? And perhaps more important, how does he or she come to that decision? Every week, thousands of features and news stories are "spiked" – left unpublished. Usually this is because they are just plain boring, or unsubstantiated or defamatory. But what about the good stuff that is not published but kept on file? Who makes the decision to kill a story before it gets off the ground?

Some years ago, before the 2001 invasion of Iraq, I spent a week or so in the NATO airbase at Insurlik in Turkey. It was mid December during the six-month run-up to an election, and the airfield was close to the border with Kurdistan. It was a bleak, miserable place, far from the soft tourist underbelly of the Mediterranean coast, and it was bitterly cold. The city of Insurlik, about ten miles from the base, was a "no-go" zone for the airmen and ground crew on the base. In part, this was because of the infamous debtor's prison. In those days, if you owed money in Turkey you went to jail until you paid the debt. If you had no money or assets of any sort, then your only choice was to sell your family into prostitution. The result was that the city was a dangerous and violent place, particularly at night, and the camp commanders enforced a ban on contact of any sort with the local population.

The base itself wasn't much safer. The Turks were in conflict with the Kurds, and Kurdish terrorist groups such as the KSA were bombing and shooting civilians in Istanbul. Although Insurlik was a NATO facility where Turkish, American, British, and French squadrons of fast ground-attack jet aircraft were based, it was obviously owned by the Turks, and the week before I arrived, they had imposed a curfew on all non-Turkish military personnel. Four days later, a Turkish sentry shot and killed an American serviceman who was out jogging at dusk on the perimeter track. It was never reported in the UK or US press.

Compared to the Americans, who slept in well-built barracks, and could eat at McDonalds and shop in the PX, which sold everything at knockdown prices, the RAF servicemen were very much the poor relations on the base. Their messes were in wooden huts and, despite the intense cold, they were forced to sleep in tents. Every day, British Tornados, American and Turkish F16s and French Mirage aircraft would leave the base in large numbers to patrol the skies over Northern Iraq and enforce the UN-imposed "no fly zone". It was a hazardous, painstaking duty during which Iraqi radar regularly locked on to the NATO aircraft to test their response.

After I had been on the base for three or four days, I began to realize that all was not well. Relations with the Turkish commander were "unsatisfactory" to say the least, and sometimes, without warning, he would bring a halt to flying from the base for anything other than Turkish Airforce activity. The Turks were well trained and well supplied with military hardware. Their American F16s were the best strike attack aircraft in the world and they had all the necessary ordnance including laser-guided bombs and Hellfire air-to-ground missiles.

RAF aircrew were extremely unhappy, but this was not because of the conditions in which they were expected to live, nor the equipment they had been given to do the job. Two days before I was due to catch the Hercules back to London, I discovered that what was upsetting the aircrew was what was happening when the Turks restricted flying to Turkish aircraft only. A senior RAF Pilot Officer told me that the Turks had recently started flying low-level missions into the mountains south and east of Al Mawsil, where they were dropping napalm onto the Kurdish villages.

The fact that NATO aircraft with NATO markings were napalming civilian settlements understandably infuriated the British servicemen and there was a great deal of anger and unrest on the base. They had aerial surveillance film of the effects of the bombings and some claimed to have witnessed it happening during patrols that were designed to confine Saddam Hussein to his air bases and keep an eye on military movements in Northern Iraq.

I duly flew back to Brize Norton at the end of the week and filed my copy and pictures to the *Mail on Sunday*. This was still in the days, not so long ago, when email was a rare luxury – and unavailable to me – and so I decided to travel straight to London and deliver everything to the newsroom. I felt that I had a serious story about seriously discontented British servicemen, Turkish brutality and the compromising of the NATO missions over Northern Iraq. I had statements from RAF officers and French pilots to back up what I had written.

The story was received in silence. "This was not actually what we wanted from you," was the response. In the end I was told to rewrite it all and produce a piece about our boys having to live in tents in the frozen wastes of Kurdistan, far from their homes and families, just as Christmas was coming. In fact, I had noticed little discontent about the tents and accommo-dation, it was the napalmed villages that was making everyone so miserable. In the end, the real story was never published. Everywhere I took it, I received the same response from editors – pursed lips and a shrugged, "sorry, not for us". I couldn't under-stand it because I felt it was a serious problem that deserved national and international publicity. It never has been published, at least not in detail. I believed at the time that this was because "Kurds and Napalm" were the antithesis of the comfortable Christmas story. I was wrong. The problems between the Kurds and Turks were a price that had to be paid by the NATO alliance and it was not considered to be in anyone's interest to raise it as an issue in the media. The revelations might eventually risk the availability of valuable military facilities and compromise NATO's ability to enforce UN resolutions. The press as a whole had agreed to toe the line and that was that.

Why is it that the print media decide to kill such stories and ignore a subject that is obviously of major national interest? There is one particular major political secret that has never been aired in public in Britain. It concerns the sexuality of a senior Labour politician who is already in high office. It is a subject that the politician concerned never discusses and yet every editor in "Fleet Street" is aware of. It is bound to be revealed one day and will have serious repercussions because it is a subject that would normally be grabbed by the tabloids and squeezed until the last drop of value has been extracted. Also, the national readership will want to know (in the public interest) why the story has been kept secret for so long. When it finally blows, the politician concerned will make a dignified riposte and the reptiles will start to turn over the stones until they have what they need, if indeed they don't have it already. It may, or may not have, long-term political repercussions. It's impossible to tell.

The question is, what considerations persuade the media to publish or reject stories such as these? In the case of the Turkish atrocities in Iraq, the press were presumably persuaded that to release the facts would not be in the national interest and could compromise some sort of operational or strategic policy. It is hard to make this opinion stand up, nowadays, but it is likely that "Turk bashing" was considered inadvisable by the government and after a quiet word from a senior minister "Fleet Street" decided to suppress the story. The second story has also been suppressed because of a request from those parties directly involved. It is not a matter of illegal behaviour. The politician concerned has simply asked that his private life should be kept quiet and out of the public gaze. When important issues don't become news or receive any attention in the press, it's often because of the political leanings of the proprietor and his executive editors or just one part of the complex web of pledges and promises that characterize relationships in the news market. Proprietors and their editors discuss stories with each other and make agreements never to rat on another proprietor.

The British general election was not only memorable for the apparent narrowness of the policies under discussion, but also because, for the first time, the political parties ran high-tech election campaigns controlled by professional and very aggressive teams of managers. The Labour and Conservative parties together spent many millions of pounds on covert and technically highly advanced campaigns in an attempt to influence the vital eight hundred thousand key voters in marginal seats who had to be converted to their cause if they were to win the election. Both parties knew that the final decision would be determined by fierce local battles fought in these marginal seats, and that the action would be away from the media. Both sides made determined efforts to identify the small sections of the electorate necessary to do this. The Conservative and Labour leaders used helicopters, when possible, to hop speedily about the countryside throughout the campaign. It was madcap canvassing carefully planned to run at great speed, and physically exhausting. Michael Howard said that it was fewer than 2 per cent of the electorate who mattered to the final result and who had to be persuaded to move away from New Labour if the Tories were to have any hope of winning an overall majority.

Much of Labour's £15 million campaign budget was spent on this battle for the marginals, fought in the key constituencies. The money was allocated to canvassing rather than press or poster advertising. The Labour National Communications Centre in Newcastle made two and a half million calls to electors in the year before the election was announced. It also posted one and a half million leaflets every month. The Conservative national call centre, at Coleshill, near Coventry, in the Midlands, was after the same voters, of course. At one stage the Tory call centre was sending out one million leaflets a day and making the same number of telephone calls. Telephone canvassing and direct mail are of little use in political elections unless the concerns of the recipients are understood and satisfied. If a voter's sole preoccupation is the gypsies who have moved into the field at the bottom of the garden, there's little point in talking to him about pensions. The million or so target voters had to be profiled and canvassed accordingly with letters or phone calls explaining the party's policies on the issues that concerned them and attacking the other party's policies.

Both political parties used "data capture" software to create databases from postcodes, library records and loyalty card databases. Before the election, the Conservatives developed the Voter Vault system to predict the likelihood that an individual voter will support them or reject them. They said it had an accuracy rating of about 75 per cent. The source of their data mining has remained a secret, although Experian and LexisNexis were both involved in advising the party, and data from the country's biggest loyalty card databases will have been acquired through data marketing companies and used in the monitoring. Similar strategies to target key groups in swing states or counties were used by the Bush Campaign in the election of 2004.

Both parties held fewer press conferences, and the Labour Party in particular, avoided what they regarded as a generally hostile press and instead chose to seek direct contact with the electorate. The only battle bus was used by the Deputy Prime minister, John Prescott. Labour, which also targeted around three quarters of a million key voters, isolated five thousand voters in all sixty of its key marginal constituencies. They mailed all of them a DVD containing messages from Tony Blair and their local Labour candidate discussing local issues. This ambitious and expensive exercise was followed up with emails to a hundred thousand voters telling them personally what the Prime Minister had been doing that week, including the fact that he had been to Buckingham Palace to ask the Queen to dissolve Parliament, thus triggering an election. He also made a daily video diary that appeared on the party website where he again discussed the "high and low points" of his day and repeated the message that it was going to be a tough campaign in which every seat would have to be fought for. While this was going on, the team controlled by Lynton Crosby, the Australian electoral mastermind, brought in to create and manage the campaign for the Conservatives, was providing the media with lists of what they claimed were the lies Blair had told the British public.

The campaign was notable for the claims and counterclaims that were made about expenditure. These were not only passed on by politicians in person, but were also released in steady drips by telephone to the media. Labour employed a team of media communicators to email and target journalists directly with stories on education and the NHS. Material of this sort is usually carefully targeted to the political writers and the parliamentary "lobby" – the special group of political journalists with privileged access to the top politicians – who rarely divulge exactly who leaked information to them. But as the campaign developed it became apparent that the targets of political spin during the election were no longer the media but had been transferred to the key marginal voters in person. The impetus for this came from Labour strategists, shaken by the public backlash over Iraq seen during the campaign. Although the national polls showed a clear Labour lead overall, the party was concerned because senior members knew that the real campaign was taking place away from the eyes of the media in the marginal constituencies.

One of Blair's leading advisers referred to a talk given more than three years previously to the National Press Club of Australia. The speaker was Lynton Crosby, who had guided John Howard's Liberal Party to a miraculous victory in the Australian general election, and was now trying to do the same for Michael Howard. Crosby pointed out to his Australian audience that many media commentators do not see much of the real campaign these days. "It does not take place on the TV, on the radio or even in newspapers. It is the local activity on the ground that really counts – letters to voters, postcards, newsletters, telephone canvassing, door-knocking ..."

Politics has changed a great deal since the 1997 election, when the Labour Party revelled in its unfamiliar status as a landslide winner in a one-sided campaign, and positively encouraged stories about the slick professionalism of its campaign's organizers, such as the media Svengali Peter Mandelson and Blair's press secretary Alastair Campbell, a hero in the PR trade. The electoral strategies taken up by the Labour and Conservative parties in 2005 were nothing new. It was the PR and marketing industry that has pioneered the manipulative techniques used by Howard and Blair. These were developed to cultivate covert influence on the media in the interests of their clients in business and business-friendly political parties such as "New Labour". Colin Byrne, head of the giant PR consultancy Weber Shandwick, was formerly a key Labour spin advisor. The Shandwick Election Guide pointed out before the election date was announced that "contrary to popular belief, the

2005 campaign will see a concentrated effort to put the grass-roots campaign in key marginal seats rather than any sort of 'presidential' national media campaign". It was to be a revolutionary change in electoral politics that would be taken up by both main parties.

Since 2001, most new thinking has been imported from the United States and, to a lesser extent, Australia. In particular, "permission marketing", long in use by business, has now crossed over into politics. "Permission marketing" involves the use of surveys, leaflets and letters to encourage the electorate to respond directly to a campaign, in other words to get "permission" from individual voters to enter into a conversation with them. By using direct contact in this way it allows the party workers to talk about the issues that the individual voter cares most about. The system was used in the 2005 election campaign by all the main political parties. The Conservatives and Labour invested heavily in software that targeted voters according to their social characteristics so that mail shots and phone calls could be directed straight towards the voters most concerned by a particular issue. In theory, this means that, for instance, home owners can be targeted with messages about issues that concern them directly, such as mortgages and stamp-duty. VoterVault, as used by the Tories, was modelled on an American system, while Labour used Labour Contact, a similar package.

None of this is visible to the general public or the media. During the start of the electioneering, as the party's website ran a story about possible party advertising campaigns, Alistair Campbell was spotted entering Labour headquarters, ready to join the campaign. One of the subsequent themes depicted Howard as Charles Dickens's "Fagin" and the media went into overdrive condemning the anti-Semitism of the image. The result, as Campbell no doubt predicted, was that the story ran and ran and provided lengthy coverage for Labour. The party issued lengthy denials about an ulterior motive, while at the same time enforcing their claim that the Conservatives would be parsimonious when it came to funding the NHS. Highlighting Howard's Jewish roots and the image of him hypnotizing the electorate with a pocket watch on a chain stuck in the mind. It was a clever tactic, although it could only be used once. The Conservatives were unable to put a stop to the story because they had no control over it. Howard was asked to comment many hundreds of times, but demurred.

The two main parties had disciplined "key seat" strategies in which they focused maximum effort on the limited number of constituencies that might change hands. They were able to deploy national telephone banks, national mail shots, full-time organizers and campaign visits by senior party members into these small battleground seats. In Labour's case, the list of key seats was leaked to the press and numbered 107 constituencies, all of which were held by Labour in 2001. In the end, the number was drastically shortened during the four weeks of the official campaign. Doorstep canvassing and the subsequent analysis of voter reactions and concerns, the use of focus groups and regular reports to HQ about what the other parties were up to was fed into the party database and processed.

The Conservatives are known to have had an internal debate early in the campaign about whether to have a "realistic" and limited number of target seats, or a more ambitious list of objectives worked out on the basis of winning an overall majority. The Liberal Democrats, who were unable to focus similar resources on their campaign, were nevertheless ruthless about their targeting and tried to follow a policy of "decapitating" or "beheading" the Conservatives – in other words targeting senior Tory party members in what they assumed to be "winnable" seats. As it turned out, the policy was unsuccessful. For the two years prior to polling day, the main parties had been carrying out voter identification surveys, leafleting campaigns and direct mail shots in their target areas. Canvassing is not necessarily intended to sway people's opinions – it is carried out so that the canvasser can identify potential supporters and gauge local attitudes to party policy. The parties then use further canvassing and direct contact up to and including polling day to make sure their known supporters will turn out and vote. Voters in marginal seats are considered priceless and the party databases are regularly updated to record their profiles so that they are targeted constantly. You would never get away with this approach if you were trying to sell double glazing rather than a political philosophy.

VoterVault, Mosaic and Labour Contact are valuable political assets and will become more important as they increase in size. Data, which comes from a variety of sources, is inputted immediately it is received at Conservative or Labour headquarters. During the 2005 election, data was donated to the Conservatives by party benefactors. The election in 2005 was decided by covert and market-oriented electioneering. One of the lasting controversies about the election – aside from the obvious issue of Iraq – will be how this covert campaign was fought, including the rise in the use of postal voting and the techniques used, which went against the advice given by the Electoral Commission. This left questions about manipulation and fraud that will have to be sorted out.

The Conservatives certainly took a risk with their 2005 electioneering techniques. They employed Crosby tactics such as "dog whistles" – sounding off on highly selective issues that are inaudible to the masses, but which will be "heard" and supported by the target groups they are trying to reach. They also launched character attacks more vicious than anything they had ever used before. While the party failed to regain power, they managed to edge themselves back into contention as a serious party following disastrous defeats at the previous two elections. However, it was certainly, by the traditional standards of "The Party of Government", a vicious and dirty campaign. Lynton Crosby was given a standing ovation when he addressed Central Office workers two days before the election. After the counting was finished, it seemed that his tactics have brought the Tories back from the dead. Crosby's machinations certainly rattled Alastair Campbell – who compiled a dossier on how the Tories have imported disreputable tactics from the United States and Australia. In a briefing to political journalists, he did his best to expose Tory "dirty tricks", a difficult task for the man who compiled the "Dodgy Dossier" on Iraq. "No one has ever tried this before in British politics," he said.

The Tories realized that, tactically, they could not promote themselves as an alternative government. Instead Crosby moulded the Tories into a vehicle to "send Blair a message". The strategy was, "Don't waste time on the policies, just attack the opposition." When Crosby arrived, he was alarmed at the paucity of the Tory policy armoury, so he told them that they could never do in six months what they should have been doing in the last six years. He got the party to adopt his "Queensland Strategy", which is to make a virtue out of a hopeless position and persuade voters that, "You will not win, so go for the Tories as a protest vote because they are not a viable alternative government." It had worked in Crosby's native Queensland in 1995, but he took the considerable risk of judging that such a negative campaign style might persuade people not to vote at all.

His other tactic, the "dog whistle" was another way of "appealing to the racists". Stung by the success of the UK Independence Party in the 2004 European Parliament elections, the Tories decided to copy UKIP's anti-immigration message, which included withdrawal from the Geneva convention on refugees, thus attracting blue-collar workers – the targets of the message. But would they outnumber the bourgeois, urban voters who might find any hint of racial politics distasteful? The answer would come in how the Tories performed in seats such as Putney, which they won. Finally, was it right to focus the campaign so much behind Michael Howard? Howard was formerly one of the most disliked Tory ministers, his turnaround has been remarkable. But was he too easy to caricature as a vampire from the dark Tory past?

"Give Tony Blair a bloody nose," said Brian Sedgemore, the long-serving Labour MP who quit Labour during the campaign because of his opposition to the war in Iraq. "Wipe the smirk off his face," demanded the Conservative spin merchants. The voters did both, to an extent, but Blair remained in power, although there was no hint of triumphalism in his victory speech. He admitted the electorate wanted to punish the Government. He even mentioned the war in Iraq, and accepted it had been divisive, saying he hoped the country could unite again. Coming at the end of a campaign in which he had been characterized as a liar, a liability to his own party, a lame duck and had been trapped by a journalist into discussing his sex life, it raised the question: Can Blair come back? He promised to step down during this Parliament, probably handing power to his Chancellor, Gordon Brown. But he didn't have to do so for at least three years.

There are many ways to read the baffling and vicious election. Between 1979 and 1992, the Labour Party lost four elections in a row, and seemed to be unelectable. Today it has shaped a new British social democracy. At the same time, its 36 per cent share of the popular vote is "the smallest of any governing party since Britain became a democracy," according to Anthony King, the political scientist. What is more, it is unclear what ideas the Labour Party has left. Blair's pledge in the 2001 campaign to make public services responsive to market forces – allowing people to choose which hospitals and schools they use – was largely derailed by the focus on Iraq. This time New Labour's campaign looked very "old" Labour, a promise not to reform but to defend services against Tory attacks – "if you value it, vote for it". But the profiling and marketing and dirty tricks practiced by both sides are what we will remember from the 2005 election. But what if someone had released all the secret information contained in the files in Northcliffe House? It would be just like opening Pandora's box...

Conclusion

These are dangerous times. We are still in involved in a
major conflict in Iraq where a "holy war" between Islam
and Christian America continues to flourish. In Baghdad, the
nurses at the Centre for the Treatment of Victims of Torture
continue to tend Iraqis whose tormentors have switched
from Saddam's secret police to CIA-backed interrogators.
There is no exit strategy for British or American troops, and
yet President Bush is now rattling his sabre and threatening
to bomb nuclear installations in Iran. How did we get to this?
Why have our leaders suddenly become so convinced that
they represent the forces of good against an evil empire?
Why do they want to take away our privacy, discover our
most personal secrets, and know our innermost thoughts?
And why don't we care enough to do something about it?

We're living in a world where virtually everything we say or do
can be recorded, intercepted, stuck in a database, analysed,
transmitted to the security services, or sold to a data marketing company. If the watchers really want to know about us, they
can use a surveillance satellite to target our movements, day or
night, inside or out, in rainstorm or fog. They may, of course, be
able to save themselves all this trouble by subscribing to one of
the international profiling companies. These guys can tell them
who your neighbours are, the numbers and balances on your

bank accounts, how much tax you pay, how much tax you avoid (or evade!), who you buy your drugs from, the names and addresses of your lovers, your social security number, criminal record, and inside leg measurement. They know all the nasty little secrets you may keep from the authorities.

What we must now accept is that we gave away our privacy years ago. We didn't make a conscious decision to abandon the right to a private life without other people sticking their noses in, it just happened. We simply waved "goodbye" to all the safeguards that our forebears had fought for, and the politicians ignored what was going on. We didn't realize that while the watchers went about learning all they could about us and turning their knowledge into a profit, we just watched television or took a holiday. So I make no excuse for beginning the final chapter of this book with a reminder of how the United Kingdom, traditionally liberal and relaxed in comparison with the United States, has changed so much.

It didn't taken long for a British Prime Minister to embrace what he described as "hard reality" and "common sense" after September 11, 2001. In 1994, Tony Blair, leader of the opposition at the time, said in the House of Commons, "The Liberty of the subject should be taken away, not by the act of a politician, but by a court of law." Nevertheless, it was a Home Secretary in Tony Blair's government who awarded himself exceptional new powers that would allow him to put under house arrest anyone he regarded as a threat, without going through a trial and conviction in a court of law. The Right Reverend Peter Selby, Bishop of Worcester, referring to this development, said, "I remain puzzled as to why the Government has felt it necessary to go down the road of an executive decision in a matter that constitutionally belongs to the judiciary." The answer is that when the country is subject to attack by an enemy, however notional, the public tends to think that "anything goes" and politicians naturally view this situation as an opportunity to extend their power. The difficulty always is getting politicians to divest themselves of their illiberal antics and return to the old system when, if ever, the threat vanishes and peace returns. I'm certainly not holding my breath. Along with civil liberties such as trial by jury and presumption of innocence until proved guilty, our right to privacy means nothing now.

Echelon, the monstrous data-gathering system sponsored by the UK and US security services and supported by nations such as Canada and Australia, is able to capture every electronic communication between the Middle East, Europe and the United States every minute of every day. It is a massive technical achievement, particularly when you realize that the data it collects has to be electronically analysed, sorted, sifted and refined until it has been reduced down to manageable material that can be evaluated by human beings. Theoretically, only data related to the strict criteria laid down by the security services can be obtained in this way, but how do we know that for sure? The Echelon software is revolutionary and has not been copied elsewhere, mostly because only the US has the resources to produce the manpower and equipment required, such as highly sophisticated military surveillance satellites and well-staffed ground-based monitoring stations. However, the French now have their own system, smaller, of course, but, like Echelon, based in space. It is the start of a race. Where did it all begin?

One month after the attack on the World Trace Center – the "Twin Towers" – the Bush administration enacted the "Patriot Act", and in the process launching the attack on civil liberties that went with it. President Bush and his supporters see their nation as "Fortress America", engaged in a global "War Against Terror" and this gave them the justification they needed to attack Afghanistan and then march into Iraq. The British Government, making use of the swarms of intelligence traffic from all over the world, rounded up suspected terrorists and imprisoned them in a gulag of high-security prisons. When, finally, the judiciary told the government that they were acting against constitutional principles, they released all the suspects before changing the constitution to allow them to put anyone they chose under house arrest without charge or trial.

The constitutional fragmentation now taking place in Britain must be set against a background of prolonged assaults on civil liberties. These assaults include not only an attack on the principals of trial by jury and the presumption of innocence until proved guilty, but also the requirement that everyone must prove they exist by paying for their own identity card. These all represent serious attempts to alter the balance of constitutional power in favour of the executive. They are demands that, even in the United States, would be rejected immediately by the Senate. The British Government took the opportunity afforded it by a massive parliamentary majority to corrupt the Civil Service, even taking power from civil servants and giving it to un-elected apparatchiks or "advisers" and going to war with Iraq on the basis of informal and questionable advice from the Attorney General. The Government got away with these abuses because of its parliamentary majority, and also because of the feel-good factor of an apparently healthy economy and the fact that not enough members of the electorate felt sufficient rage to unseat it.

The most significant loss of liberty, which has come about almost unnoticed by the voting public, is the pernicious and constant level of surveillance that has crept into the day-to-day life of everyone in Britain. The electorate hardly notices it because voters are more concerned with taxation, local government, central government, immigration and regulation. But the time will come when they will realize that their liberty, once the most valuable prize of all, has gone for ever.

The loss of privacy did not come about through the decisions of politicians alone, it has also resulted from the activities of commerce, and it is a fact that there is now a massive international marketplace for information in which data can be sold, exchanged and bartered for all over the world, despite the safeguards supposedly laid down in the Data Protection Act and the Freedom of Information Act. In the world of the "web", the data marketing companies have to operate in an international arena to have any hope of financial success. The big players competing against each other and using our life histories as their raw material are too rich and powerful for tin-pot politicians to legislate against in any meaningful way.

The market in information will flourish because there are databases everywhere. The National Health Service database contains the medical histories of everyone in the United Kingdom. It seems sad that the conversion of all this data into computerized form spells the end of those old card indexes containing the jottings of family doctors in their traditionally indecipherable handwriting. The indexed cards with ancient smudges, coffee stains and strange hieroglyphics, complicated chemical formulae, intimate details of a family's sex life, their diseases, painful accidents and embarrassing genito-urinary ailments have all been translated into computer language somehow. The doctors' euphemisms, often written in code ("PFO" universally stands for "pissed, fell over") all noted down in fountain pen, ball point or sometimes pencil have become obsolete now that they have been transcribed onto a massive database, which will be open to "accredited" members of the National Health Service.

The fact is that the potential for inaccuracies will be massive and the consequential health risks serious. It is what the Government describes as "progress", but it is the loss of control over this priceless private resource that is most worrying. The very fact that it exists means the staff at the hospital where you are admitted to have your prostate removed or your wisdom teeth extracted will be able to gain access to your private history. As a direct consequence of the growth in the data mining industry, some of those privileged to have access to this sort of confidential data will be offered huge incentives to sell it to those who can make the most of it. This includes countless government ministers, health administrators, consultants, nurses, GPs and paramedics, who will have easy access to your personal details, even if it means going against their code of practice.

Health will soon be joined by education. School records from local education authorities will be annotated and transferred onto a Department for Education database. What will go on it? Attendance records, detentions, homework marks and test results? Private opinions from disaffected teachers or school inspectors? Will this information be made available to potential employers who may be tempted to base their opinions on a teacher's opinion of an applicant's character, assessed when he or she was twelve years old? We all change as time goes on. We mature and we develop physically, mentally and emotionally. Our growth and development is, of course, subject to events. Data, as it comes out of a computer, is as desiccated as a skeleton in the desert. It relies on analysis, often carried out automatically by the computer software, to add flesh to the bare bones. The fact that, in its raw form, the data is being collected in huge quantities without our permission and without any real safeguards to prevent it from falling into the wrong hands, is acutely worrying.

Nothing holds more true than these three little words: "knowledge is power", and it is an obvious fact that all politicians accept this without question. Yet there is no meaningful legislation to protect us from the misuse of our private details. The Data Protection Act does little to stop the executive from collecting and holding knowledge about our lives. Surely the protection should come before the collection?

The nagging doubt at the back of my mind is, how secure will my health and education histories be? It is important to me because I don't necessarily want some insurance broker to know that I had rheumatic fever as a child (which I didn't), or that I was expelled from school for taking drugs when I was fifteen (which I wasn't), or that I had an appointment in the Praed Street VD clinic after discovering an angry-looking boil when I was eighteen (which I might have). But worse than the potential loss of privacy and confidentiality, is the knowledge that the NHS database will be one of the most complex pieces of data mining ever attempted. Its privacy is vital to all those in the UK who value the sanctity of their private life. Yet it is the responsibility of politicians and civil servants to ensure that not a single item of health information gets into the wrong hands. It is a hopeless task. There will be all sorts of legislation and promises of dire retribution against anyone caught hacking into the data, but the drugs and insurance industries are multi-national and the value of a nation's health records is inestimable.

The same applies to education. Why should the personal and highly subjective opinions of men and women made years ago be available today without the permission of the person whom they concern? My fear is that it will be a matter of months rather than years before the life histories of large numbers of the British population will be in the hands of drug companies and others with the wherewithal to pay for them.

When this happens the media, ever eager to learn something explicit and personal about the public, will lose any inhibitions they might have had about the misuse of personal data, if it means they can get their hands on the details of a rock singer's drug rehabilitation history or sexual behaviour at school.

Databases are a product of joined-up government. Once identity card information is pooled and cross-referenced with other personal data, including Inland Revenue and Customs and Excise records, Criminal Records, the new and fast-growing Police facial recognition database, the NHS database, the huge amount of knowledge gained and stored from smart cards and credit cards, immigration records, the Department for Education database, the Passport Office, driving licences, bank records, library records and the National Register of Births, Marriages and Deaths, everything about us will be known – and that's probably more than we know about ourselves.

Unless the public rebel against the misuse of information that already exists in the UK and the US, massive database like this will exist within the next twenty years. The simple identity card will be overtaken by a State-owned life history of every one of us. The data will be inaccurate and its existence is profoundly illiberal. Nevertheless, our cyber-files will be used to form judgments about us and could become the basis of a police state. The US has shown the way with its CAPPS11 programme, designed to profile the entire population in order to identify potential terrorists on airline passenger lists. When you know as much as it is possible to know about a population, and it is stored electronically, you can begin to draw conclusions from all the knowledge you have collected. Cross-referencing and personality profiling are already common. It is not difficult to imagine the dreadful consequences of the technology in the hands of a seriously repressive state.

Data mining will continue and the intelligence services will grow increasingly powerful and add sauce to the potent mix of information gained from public records. MI5 and MI6, the two arms of the British Secret Service, are responsible respectively for national and international intelligence. Both services have been on their highest level of alert – "Severe" (general) – since November 2003, when Al Qaeda bombed the British Consulate building in Istanbul, killing the Consul General and twenty-five others. "High alert" means that a terrorist attack is expected on the British Mainland and all the specialist anti-terrorist units of the police, secret service, military and emergency services must be permanently on standby. MI5, the domestic security service, has its base a quarter of a mile up river from Parliament, at Thames House, near the Tate Gallery. The Director General, Eliza Manningham-Buller, a crusty, career spook, has had to take the blame for the failures of intelligence during the build-up to war with Iraq. Both MI5 and MI6 have been subjected to sweeping reforms since the claim that weapons of mass destruction could be targeted at Britain within forty-five minutes was made by Prime Minister Tony Blair to justify his decision to go to war. The security services have also been accused of identifying Dr David Kelly, the chemical weapons expert who took his life during the furore over the revelation that the "dodgy dossier" that supposedly detailed Saddam's weapons capability had in fact been "sexed up". It was obvious that something had to be done after the Lord Butler's report stated that MI6 had misread Saddam Hussein's weapons capabilities.

The reform of British intelligence came in a typically vague announcement, listing new standards of reporting and error checking, the appointment of a new Head of Intelligence Analysis to oversee the work of the spies, and a "Whistleblower's Charter" to allow analysts worried that intelligence is being "overcooked" to reveal their doubts without fear of repercussions that might damage their careers. An Agencies "Staff Counsellor" has also been recruited and will be available for analysts and officials to talk to if they are unhappy with the way material is being used. More analysts have been recruited into MI6 and "standardized terms" have been adopted to describe the reliability of secret sources. However, the British government accepted that the dossier prepared as part of the justification for going to war with Iraq was faulty and that any future report like that should clearly separate ministerial views from the assessment of the Joint Intelligence Committee.

It seems strange that our spies are being so carefully monitored and regulated and their behaviour brought up to scratch by the state while the politicians who made the allegations about the forty-five minute chemical munitions threat remain above all criticism. While the Foreign Secretary was announcing the reforms to the intelligence services, and how they must go about reporting secret information from now on, MI5, which has several hundred officers permanently involved in anti-terrorist activity, was recruiting one thousand new staff in the UK. It has also established a network of local "desks" to keep an eye on regional threats. The numbers of people employed in spying on the British public is growing all the time, and while their activities are naturally kept secret, they have become more visible and powerful in recent years. In London, SO13, the police anti-terrorist group, employs nine hundred Special Branch (SO12) and anti-terrorist branch (SO13) officers, while fifteen hundred more have been deployed in regional forces in the West Midlands, Manchester and Scotland. The elite army surveillance unit, the 14 Intelligence Company, which has spent many years monitoring Republican and Loyalist terrorist cells in Northern Ireland, has been relocated to provide assistance to the specialist military regiments, such as the SAS and SBS, in their future operations outside the UK. The unit is now known as the Special Reconnaissance Regiment and is stationed at Hereford (also home to the SAS). The regiment's job is to provide covert surveillance of terrorist organizations before special forces operations are carried out. It is one of the most respected regiments in the British military forces and its likely posting to Iraq comes at the direct request of the American Military. It is a small unit of less than one hundred men and women and their experience in surveillance, learned the bloody way on the streets of Belfast, is considered unique.

The increase in manpower employed in spying and intelligence on the British mainland has clearly been introduced in response to what is perceived as an identifiable threat. But Eliza Manningham-Buller declines to say just how big a threat that is. In particular, she refuses to quote numbers because she believes that, as well as there being a small band of dedicated terrorists on the mainland, there is also an indeterminate number of passive sympathizers who may or may not provide support, but who would turn a blind eye to the terrorist activities of others if asked. One unofficial MI5 source has estimated that up to three thousand young British Muslims attended the Al Qaeda training camps before the camps were closed down in 2002. Lord Hoffman, the Law Lord who reviewed the suspects detained without trial at Belmarsh, believes the figure to be closer to one thousand.

Small pieces of information are released by the security services on an occasional basis, such as the fact that the Joint Terrorism Analysis Centre at Thames House has received sixty thousand pieces of intelligence about an imminent attack and that the attack, when and if it comes, will be a conventional assault by a suicide bomber during a significant time such as a general election or the State Opening of Parliament. But it is in the nature of Al Qaeda that they strike at unexpected times and at unpredictable targets. Osama Bin Laden is a brilliant strategist and has time on his hands. At an international summit on "Democracy, Terrorism and Security", held in Madrid in March 2005, it was stressed that it was vital to fight terrorism without compromising freedom. A concluding statement said that the law enforcement agencies need the powers to do the job but they must never sacrifice the principles they are dedicated to defending.

The trouble is that the intelligence services have never really accepted that they should play a part in the criminal process and much of what they do goes unrecorded. In the opinion of the professional spook, suspicion should be sufficient to have someone locked up. The intelligence services are always reluctant to produce "evidence" in case it compromises their sources. Their activities should never be exposed to the dissection and minute examination of a Crown court trial, they believe. The interception of telephone calls was illegal in Britain until the mid-1980s. You could only carry out wiretaps if you applied for, and were granted, a warrant by the Home Secretary. To qualify, the interception had to be part of an on-going investigation into a serious crime or to do with safeguarding the security of the State, and even then, only if the information could not be obtained any other way. But then the rules were relaxed. Immediately there were stories of misbehaviour by MI5 agents, who, in addition to snooping on Iron Curtain Embassies and consular offices, started to pry into trade unions and organizations such as the Campaign for Nuclear Disarmament (CND). This had nothing to do with the legal process. MI5 was not trying to build a legal case, it was just gathering intelligence and building up a picture to show it "knew what was going on".

There was never the slightest suggestion that any of the conversations MI5 recorded would be used in court.

A ruling by the European Court of Human Rights forced the Government to pass the Interception of Communications Act (1985), which laid out the criteria for legal intercepts. However, it excluded the courts from any involvement. One section of the Act stated that during proceedings before a court, no evidence was to be adduced and no questions were to be asked in cross-examination that might suggest that an interception had taken place, with or without a warrant. This was included in the Act because the security services were worried that their previously illegal, but now quiet lawful, wiretapping activities might be referred to during court proceedings and that their continuing illegal operations might be held against them. Even in cases involving national security, evidence from wiretaps is inadmissible. The judiciary disapprove of the security services being excluded because it insulates the spies from the legal process. The judges also resent the fact that the Government supported the decision. The police, the Department of Public Prosecutions, the pressure group Liberty and the Joint Parliamentary Committee on Human Rights have all condemned the restriction as "ridiculous". George Churchill-Coleman, a former head of the anti-terrorist squad at Scotland Yard, remarked that Britain was sinking into a police state. "The refusal of the intelligence services to yield on the admissibility of intercept evidence and the support they have received for their position from their political masters is the clearest evidence we have that if [it] is not yet the case [that Britain is a police state], it is the wish of important elements in our political and security community."

The British security services are accountable only to an all-powerful executive, which has proved time and again that it is able and willing to pry and poke into our privacy. As MI5 and

MI6 grow bigger, and the nation's databases proliferate, the gloomy warnings about future terrorist outrages will be repeated until, despite little evidence of a serious terrorist threat, we will begin to worry more about our safety than our privacy. Ex army, navy and airforce men and women rarely see any conflict with civil liberties in carrying an identity card, as they had to keep one about their persons throughout their military careers. Many civilians, in all walks of life and from all backgrounds, also see little to fear from a simple piece of plastic. Of course, it is not the identity card alone that poses a major threat to civil liberties, but the proliferation of all the other infringements on our privacy, such as surveillance cameras, and international databases, together with lively and powerful security and police services now provided with all the resources they need to fight terrorism. Add to this the political will to keep tabs on everyone in Britain and America, and the frightening speed at which technology is moving, and the warning signs start to appear.

The US listening station at Menwith Hill and the UK's electronic spying facility at GCHQ in Cheltenham have between them the ability to monitor all telephone calls, emails and all other electronic communications transmitted within and passing through the British Isles. If they *can* do it, they *will* do it. Of course, there are not enough personnel to monitor everything that is being communicated, and anyway, most of it is irrelevant to those who might be interested (which might include the Inland Revenue, the police and even Tesco). But the software exists to analyse all communications and flag up relevant material for whoever might be cleared to receive it. Key words and phrases, suspect sources, destinations and languages can all be identified in raw data and brought to the attention of security agencies. The software and computing ability is constantly improving and the resources have been made available because the desperate thirst for knowledge grows stronger every day.

The CIA, aware of the fluidity of human movement throughout Europe and the Middle East, has massive computing power with which it constantly reviews and updates its lists of those it regards as "suspicious". The CIA's database of suspects contains six thousand names and is collated using wide-ranging criteria, including travel patterns, place of birth, and even name and location of relatives. This list of names is multinational and monitored electronically in the US, Britain and mainland Europe. British security services are constantly being urged to inform US agencies of any suspect behaviour in the United Kingdom by any of the names on the list.

George Friedman, the founder of Stratfor, a highly respected, independent, US-based intelligence gathering agency, believes the problem with the UK and US security services is their tendency to rely on data and "sources, rather than powerful insight". He says secret sources and databases can be referred to and quoted in support of an analysis, while an idea cannot. If a judgment is made without an established source and it goes wrong, it means that a systematic mistake has been made – and that means trouble. The CIA and MI5 are rigorously accurate in small issues and tend to be completely wrong in the things that really matter. The CIA headquarters at Langley, Virginia, is full of men who claim to have predicted 9/11. It is true that, prior to the disaster, an exercise was run in which Arab Terrorists crashed commercial aircraft into the Twin Towers. But it was one of hundreds of possible scenarios and was not taken seriously. The CIA's theory that Al Qaeda was a global conspiracy targeting the United States was based on insight, rather than evidence and information from sources. When sources told CIA agents that Al Qaeda agents were operating in a certain

European City, they could base their analysis on that piece of information and use it in briefings. For some days after 9/11, the CIA had no idea whether the US and the West was at war, or dealing with a gang of criminals.

The flash of insightful genius is rare and unwelcome at Langley and is frowned upon at Thames House. The result is that CIA and MI5 do well on the minutiae but badly on the bigger picture. Agents and officials rely on the accumulation and analysis of human intelligence and facts contained in databases to make their judgments, and they are permanently aware of what their political masters would prefer them to say in their briefings.

The next decade will see either a massive increase in the amount of intelligence about us collected and kept by the State, or a sudden rebellion against intrusion into our personal lives. I believe that there will be a struggle in which the public and civil liberties groups attempt to rein back the politicians and commercial organizations who see human beings as marketing tools and consequently exploit us and send us to work to make money or cast votes. There is no honour or public benefit to be derived from this. In her nineties, my mother, a widow living out her old age in sheltered accommodation, received regular packages of mail from finance companies. She enjoyed it because it was contact with the outside world. The letters were always unsolicited and clearly directed at the vulnerable. I used to talk to her about them and then take them away and burn them. The nursing home eventually banned junk mail when an elderly resident gave away most of his fortune after receiving one such unsolicited letter. Knowledge is power, but it also requires responsibility. We need adequate legislation to ensure the responsible use of knowledge in order to prevent the exploitation of the vulnerable.

Why don't we do something now to stop this infringement on our civil liberties? The law relating to privacy needs radical reform. When the identity card debate eventually returns to Parliament, it may be our last opportunity to throw it out for good. And while we are about it we can call for a spring clean of all those dirty corners in government and commerce where our secrets are stored so that they can be piled into computers and used against us more efficiently. A first step may be to break up the state and commercial monopolies that store knowledge about the electorate without building in any controls. Most important of all, we need new legislation that enshrines our rights to privacy, allowing us to live our lives away from State and commercial snooping. Then, perhaps, the freedoms we thought were our birthright but which are being taken away from us by stealth will be safeguarded once and for all.

Bibliography and Resources

Ball, Kirstie S. and Webster, Frank, *The Intensification of Surveillance: Crime, Terrorism and Warfare in the Information Age*, Pluto Press Ltd, 2003

Berkowitz, Bruce D. and Goodman, Allen E., *Best Truth: Intelligence in the Information Age*, Yale University Press, 2002

Brin, David G., *The Transparent Society: Will Technology Force Us to Choose Between Privacy and Freedom?*, Perseus Books, 1999

Corbin, Jane, *The Base: Al-Qaeda and the Changing Face of Global Terror*, Pocket Books, 2003

Dearnley, James and John Feather, *The Wired World: An Introduction to the Theory and Practice of the Information Society*, Library Association, 2001

Denning, Dorothy E., *Information Warfare and Security*, Addison Wesley, 1999

Drakos, Peter and John Braithwaite, *Information Feudalism: Who Owns the Knowledge Economy*, Earthscan Publications, 2002

Feather, John, *The Information Society: A Study of Continuity and Change*, Facet Publishing, 2004

Frank, Mitch, *Understanding September 11th: Answering Questions about the Attack on America*, Viking Books, 2002

Garfinkel, Simpson, *Database Nation: The Death of Privacy in the 21st Century*, O'Reilly UK, 2001

Garland, David, *The Culture of Control: Crime and Social Order in Contemporary Society*, Oxford University Press, 2002

Lessig, Lawrence, *Free Culture: How Big Media Uses Technology and the Law to Lock Down Culture and Control Creativity*, Penguin USA, 2004

Levin, Thomas Y., *CTRL (Space): Rhetorics of Surveillance from Bentham to Big Brother*, MIT Press, 2002

Lyon, David, *Surveillance After September 11*, Blackwell Publishing, 2003

Lyon, David, *Surveillance as Social Sorting: Privacy, Risk, and Automated Discrimination*, Routledge, 2002

Lyon, David, *Surveillance Society: Monitoring Everyday Life*, Open University Press, 2001

Mackey, Chris and Greg Miller, *The Interrogator's War: Inside the Secret War Against Al-Qaeda*, John Murray, 2004

McGrath, John, *Loving Big Brother: Surveillance Culture and Performance Space*, Routledge, 2004

O'Harrow, Robert, *No Place to Hide*, Free Press, 2005

Parker, John, *Total Surveillance: Investigating the Big Brother World of E-spies, Evesdroppers and CCTV*, Piatkus, 2001

Rai, Milan, *Regime Unchanged: Why the War in Iraq Changed Nothing*, Pluto

Press, 2003

Ramesh, Randeep, *The War We Could Not Stop: The Real Story of the Battle for Iraq*, Faber and Faber, 2003

Riddell, Peter, *Hug Them Close: Blair, Clinton, Bush and the "Special Relationship"*, Politicos, 2004

Riddell, Peter, *The Hidden Hand: Britain, America and Cold War Secret Intelligence*, John Murray, 2002

Ritter, Scott, *War on Iraq: What Team Bush Doesn't Want You to Know*, Profile Books, 2002

Schulsky, Abram M. and Gary J. Schmitt (ed. Gary J. Schmitt), *Silent Warfare: Understanding the World of Intelligence*, Brassey's US, 2002

Sifry, Micah L. and Christopher Cerf (eds.), *The Iraq War Reader: History, Documents, Opinions*, Touchstone Books, 2003

Silvers, Robert B. and Barbara Epstein, *Striking Terror: America's New War*, New York Review of Books, 2002

Simpson, John, *The Wars Against Saddam: Taking the Hard Road to Baghdad*, Macmillan, 2003

Stauber, John, *Weapons of Mass Deception*, Constable and Robinson, 2003

Stothard, Peter, *30 Days: A Month at the Heart of Blair's War*, HarperCollins, 2003

Todd, Paul and Jonathan Bloch, *Global Intelligence: The World's Secret Services Today*, Zed Books, 2003

Webster, Frank, *Theories of the Information Society*, Routledge, 2002

Webster, Frank and Ensio Puoskari, *The Information Society Reader*, Routledge, 2003

Woodward, *Plan of Attack*, Simon and Schuster, 2004

Civil Liberties Groups

There are hundreds of Civil Liberty organizations dealing with invasion of privacy. Most have their headquarters in Britain or the US with branches overseas. Organizations like Privacy International and Liberty deal with the problems of state surveillance, loyalty cards, Radio Bar codes, etc., and are effective and professional. In the US there are many local and national groups working away at the human rights implications of the Patriot Act, which is anti-terrorist legislation unique to the United States.

The strange passivity with which the British have submitted to the assault on their civil liberties and become the most watched nation in the world might lead us to believe that nobody really cares very much. Perhaps the public is complacent and has swallowed the politician's argument that "if you've got nothing to hide, you've got nothing to worry about"? Maybe something will occur that will make them sit up and realize what is happening. Or maybe not. The same applies to the Patriot Act and the public acceptance in America that a war is being waged against al-Qaeda, and that "anything goes."

Here is a brief list of websites for prominent civil liberty groups who are actively campaigning about the civil rights issues raised in this book. Private intelligence organizations tend to be just that – private. In spite of this, I recommend any of the "Global Intelligence Reports and Analysis" from Stratfor or the book America's Secret War by George Friedman, the founder of the company.

Amnesty International www.amnesty.org.uk
Amnesty is a worldwide voluntary movement of people who campaign for human rights. It is independent of government, political ideology, economic interest, or religion. Amnesty promotes awareness of the values contained in the Universal Declaration of Human Rights and other internationally agreed standards. It encourages all governments to ratify (agree to be bound by) and enforce international standards of human rights and, through education activities, puts pressure on governments and other political bodies (such as armed opposition groups) to support and respect human rights. It also encourages non-governmental organizations, groups, businesses, financial institutions, and individuals (sometimes called "non-state actors") to do the same. Amnesty undertakes research and action to prevent grave abuses of the rights to physical and mental integrity, freedom of conscience and expression, and freedom from discrimination.

Campaign for Nuclear Disarmament (CND) www.cnduk.org
CND campaigns non-violently to rid the world of nuclear weapons and other weapons of mass destruction and to "create genuine security for future generations."

The Electronic Frontier Foundation www.eff.org
The Electronic Frontier Foundation is a group of passionate people – lawyers, technologists, volunteers, and visionaries – "working in the trenches, battling to protect the rights of web surfers everywhere." The EFF challenges legislation that "threatens to put a price on what is invaluable; to control what must remain boundless."

Electronic Privacy Information Center (EPIC) www.epic.org
EPIC is a public interest research centre in Washington, D.C. It was

established in 1994 to focus public attention on emerging civil liberties issues and to protect privacy, the First Amendment, and constitutional values. EPIC publishes an award-winning email and online newsletter on civil liberties in the information age – the EPIC Alert. It also publishes reports and books about privacy, open government, free speech, and other important topics related to civil liberties.

Foundation for Information Policy Research www.fipr.org

GeneWatch www.genewatch.org
GeneWatch UK is a not-for-profit group that monitors developments in genetic technologies from a public interest, environmental protection, and animal welfare perspective. GeneWatch believes people should have a voice in whether or how these technologies are used and campaigns for safeguards. It works on all aspects of genetic technologies – from GM crops and foods to genetic testing of humans.

Human Rights Watch www.hrw.org
Human Rights Watch (HRW) is an independent, non-governmental organization, supported by contributions from private individuals and foundations worldwide. It accepts no government funds, directly or indirectly. HRW is dedicated to protecting the human rights of people around the world. It stands with victims and activists to prevent discrimination, uphold political freedom, protect people from inhumane conduct in wartime, and bring offenders to justice. HRW investigates and exposes human rights violations and holds abusers accountable, it challenges governments and those who hold power to end abusive practices and respect international human rights law, and it enlists the public and the international community to support the cause of human rights for all.

Internet Civil Rights campaigners

Cyber Rights & Cyber Liberties (UK)
http://www.cyber-rights.org
Centre For Criminal Justice Studies, University of Leeds, LS2 9JT
email: lawya@cyber-rights.org +44 (0) 498 865 116

Campaign Against Censorship of the Internet in Britain
http://www.liberty.org.uk
60 Albert Court, Prince Consort Road, London SW7 2BE
email: cacib@liberty.org.uk
+44 (0) 171 589 4500

Internet Freedom
www.netfreedom.org/
BM CAM, London WC1N 3XX, UK
email: campaign@netfreedom.org
+44 (0) 171 681 1559

Liberty www.liberty-human-rights.org.uk
Liberty is one of the UK's leading human rights and civil liberties organizations. It was founded as the National Council for Civil Liberties in 1934 and has campaigned for equal rights for over seventy years.

Patriot Act campaigns

American Civil Liberties Union www.aclu.org

Bill of Rights Defense Committee www.bordc.org

Privacy International www.privacyinternational.org
Privacy International (PI) is a human rights group formed in 1990 as a watchdog on surveillance and privacy invasions by governments and corporations. PI is based in London, England, and has an office in Washington, D.C. It has conducted campaigns and research throughout the world on issues ranging from wiretapping and national security, to ID cards, video surveillance, data matching, medical privacy, and freedom of information and expression.

Statewatch www.poptel.org.uk/statewatch

Stratfor www.Strafor.com

Yorkshire Campaign for Nuclear Disarmament www.cndyorks.gn.apc.org
The two key UK bases necessary for missile defence are both located in Yorkshire (Menwith Hill near Harrogate and Fylingdales near Whitby). Yorkshire CND has built up a wealth of knowledge and expertise on the subject and produced a variety of campaign resources and briefings about it. As well as campaigning regionally, Yorkshire CND works closely with the National CND office on the campaign against missile defence and the weaponization of space. Representatives of Yorkshire CND have spoken on missile defence and space issues on the national and international stage including at conferences in Geneva, Brussels, and San Francisco. Working with local groups and NGOs, Yorkshire CND "campaigns to raise awareness of the threats posed to Yorkshire, the UK and to international stability by missile defence and the ongoing push toward weapons in space".

Index